This book is presented to

_____

by

_____

Dream Big!

The Ultimate Dream

The Ultimate Dream

A Child's Gift-Giving Journey

Heather Chabino
and
Sherri Watson

Brown Books Publishing Group
Dallas, Texas

The Ultimate Dream
A Child's Gift-Giving Journey

Scripture quotations are taken from the Holy Bible, 21st Century King James Version, copyright 1994 by Deuel Enterprises, Inc.

Manufactured in the United States of America.

For information, please contact:
Brown Books Publishing Group
16200 North Dallas Parkway, Suite 170
Dallas, Texas 75248
www.brownbooks.com
972-381-0009

A New Era in Publishing™

ISBN-13: 978-1-934812-33-4
ISBN-10: 1-934812-33-1

LCCN: 2008943330
1 2 3 4 5 6 7 8 9 10

Heather dedicates this book

to her children—Kenzie and Luke. You are and

always will be a priceless gift to me!

Sherri dedicates this book to her sons

Brandon and Bradon. Thank you for making my being a

mother the best dream I have ever experienced.

You are definitely gifts from God.

I love you both very much.

Acknowledgments

Heather's Acknowledgments:

If someone had told me two years ago that I would be publishing a book, I probably would have laughed. However, I have learned a great lesson in life: I have no control over what tomorrow will bring. I started this journey with prayer, and the prayers have turned into a wonderful, never-ending journey. At the age of thirty-five, I learned that God has a plan for everyone, and in those plans, great blessings are waiting. What started as a manuscript that was written in seven days has become, a year and a half later, this wonderful gift.

I would like to thank God for allowing me to be a passenger on this incredible ride. Every single day has been a surprise. I feel honored to be on His team.

Without my best friend, my husband, I would not have been able to accomplish this. His continued patience, love, and support have been a great gift. I love you, Doug.

My children, Kenzie and Luke, "thank you" will never be enough. I have cherished every one of the hugs, and your words of love and cheers of encouragement have made this journey a delight to travel. I love you both with all my heart.

To my family, thank you for always believing in my dreams. The endless support and edification you have given during the joys and trials of life have been more than anyone can ask for. Your faith in me has been a driving force in my life, helping me accomplish many great things.

One of the richest blessings of writing this book has been getting to know Mr. Jim Stovall. I have never met a man more humble and grateful for the gifts in his life. Thank you, Jim, for everything. I would also like to acknowledge his staff—Beth, Dorothy, and Kelley—for their kindness.

To my coauthor and great friend, Sherri, I owe you the deepest gratitude for teaching me to "breathe" when things get tough and for your continuous faith. You have believed in me unremittingly since the seventh grade when I first stepped on the basketball court. I never won a state championship, but this is so much better! Now I can finally say, "We did it!"

A big thank-you to Brown Books Publishing Group and my publishing team—especially Milli Brown, Kathryn Grant, Dr. Janet Harris, Jayme Durant, Bill Young, Jessica Kinkel, and Rachel Felts—for helping turn the dream of my book into a beautiful reality. Cindy Birne and Cathy Williams are the best PR team that I could ever ask for.

A special thanks to all the volunteers and those involved with the nonprofit organizations who gave their time to be gift-givers in Kenzie's journey.

Last but never least, my sincere thanks to my friends, who have become like family. I am honored to have you all in my life. Thank you for your prayers, your encouragement, and your support. My prayer is that we will continue to "storm the gates" with His message and that we will all truly know how very blessed we are, recognizing the many gifts that fill our lives.

Sherri's Acknowledgments:

I would like to thank God for the amazing path He lays before us, for carrying me when I have strayed off of mine, and for loving me no matter what. I am very thankful He gave Heather and me this opportunity to share His love with others. How blessed we are! This journey would not have been possible without the help of many, to each of whom I would like to extend my personal and sincere thanks.

To Heather, thank you for the opportunity to be part of such an inspirational project. Our never-ending journey as friends has continued to grow over the years and will only get better in the future. I look forward to seeing what God has in store for us. I was blessed getting to share the dreams in your heart and placing them on paper.

Next, to Jim Stovall, who has been such a gift to us. Thank you for your time, patience, and inspiration.

And to Brown Books Publishing Group, especially Milli Brown, Kathryn Grant, Dr. Janet Harris, and Rachel Felts. Thank the Lord you are all patient! Thanks for allowing me to dream big and turning my dream into a reality. You will always have a special place in my heart.

Thanks to my friends, who have been so patient and supportive in reading and rereading the manuscript. Knowing you believed in me and would be there in the end pushed me harder. Hang on—this ride is just beginning.

Also to my immediate and extended family, who know me the best and love me anyway. Your support and patience in all my endeavors have given me the faith to continue. I am thankful we are so close and have each other. You are all such a blessing to me.

And thanks to my mother, for the guidance and example she and my dad placed in front of me. Your love for God was evident in our home. The love, guidance, and discipline that you both provided gave me the strength I have needed in life. I learned to dream big knowing you believe in me.

And most of all to my sons, Brandon and Bradon. Both of you have always been my driving force and a blessing only God could have created. We have been through much together, yet our bond always grows stronger. Thank you for your patience and unconditional love through the losses we have experienced and the laughs we have shared. You are truly my love and life, and I am proud of both of you. Keep looking up to God and dream big.

Contents

Foreword

When I wrote *The Ultimate Gift*, I hoped it would touch countless people who would, in turn, impact their family and friends. More than five million copies sold around the world, reflecting the longing for substance and meaning in a world that promotes acquiring "presents" instead of valuing genuine "gifts." In *The Ultimate Dream: A Child's Gift-Giving Journey*, Heather Chabino and Sherri Watson demonstrate the impact of true gift-giving on one child's life and, by extension, on all those who contributed or were touched along her path.

Heather Chabino contacted me several years ago with a level of excitement about *The Ultimate Gift* that would be hard to describe. She was determined to provide an "ultimate gift" experience for her daughter. We live in a world where unfortunately, when all is said and done, there's a lot said and very little done; however, Heather is the kind of person who makes things happen. The journey she created for her daughter has taken *The Ultimate Gift* beyond my wildest dreams.

I hope as you read these pages you will not only experience what Heather did for her daughter but also begin to think about ultimate gift experiences for yourself and those you love. Writing a book is the literary equivalent of having offspring. An author's greatest hope is that the book somehow exceeds personal accomplishments and goes places you have not been and touches people you have never met. *The Ultimate Dream: A Child's Gift-Giving Journey* extends the impact of a worldwide consciousness of how true gift-giving can make a difference—one gift and one child at a time.

I wish you happy reading and a life that becomes your own ultimate gift.

Jim Stovall
Author of *The Ultimate Gift* and
The Ultimate Life

Preface
Our Journey to the Gifts

"Aha" moments invade each of our lives at different times and in a variety of ways. My "aha" moment came in the form of Jim Stovall's book *The Ultimate Gift*. For the previous five years, I had struggled to find my purpose in life. From outward appearances, I had a good marriage, two great kids, a nice house—all the things that looked like success. However, I knew deep in my soul that God had planted big dreams in my heart, and I needed to find a way to release them. Stovall's book showed me how to unleash those dreams.

The Ultimate Gift inspired me to see life through new eyes—recognizing that lasting gifts are everywhere, and that gift-giving encompasses more than doling out material goods. Gift-giving embraces character development through bestowing treasures that can't be held by human hands. *The Ultimate Dream: A Child's Gift-Giving Journey* offers the chance to become great by partaking in transcendent gifts—the gifts of giving, learning, family, work, friends, dreams, and the ultimate gift of a relationship with God.

Our journey began under the inspiration of Jim Stovall's novel—his book propelled me into the world of true gift-giving. As I began to envision the possibilities for my family and the world around us, I put together a plan to implement gift-giving the "Stovall way." Working with my husband Doug and my dear friend and mentor Sherri Watson, we together orchestrated a journey for my daughter Kenzie—an experience that turned out to be life changing for everyone involved. I share our story with you in the hope that you too will be impacted by this gift-giving journey.

This book, *The Ultimate Dream: A Child's Gift-Giving Journey,* shares our story while offering practical tips for parents and families who want to implement a plan to change their perspectives and ultimately, their lives. We share our journey with you as an illustration of how one family—ours—put into practice true gift-giving, and we also share thirty gift-giving principles to help as you embark on your own gift-giving journey.

My desire is to give parents everywhere a vision of how they can influence their children for a lifetime and to provide the tools to get them started on their journey to giving. Changing the way we view gifts and gift-giving is the beginning of that journey. Recognizing and seeking gifts along the way enables us to make a difference in nurturing our children's lives. When we develop eyes to see the gifts around us, we begin to understand what this life is all about and the real meaning of a gift. We experience the passion of leaving a legacy for those who come after us.

Everyone comes into our lives for a reason—no meeting is accidental. Divine appointments make up the "coincidences" we encounter. I believe the reason we enter other people's lives is to bless them, and others enter our lives to bolster our weak areas and to add fullness and beauty we wouldn't possess otherwise. Greatness exists in the world around us, and we have the opportunity and privilege to share in it.

Reading Stovall's *The Ultimate Gift* was my divine appointment—my "aha" moment. Let this book—*The Ultimate Dream: A Child's Gift-Giving Journey*—be yours. Be blessed, my friend, as you discover your ultimate dream.

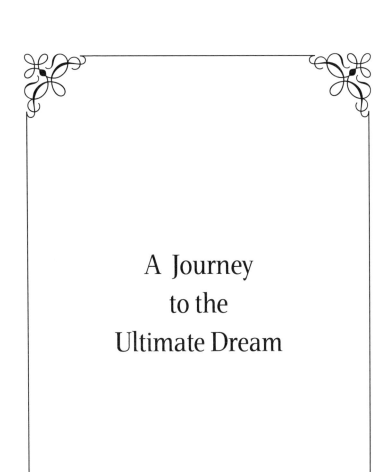

A Journey
to the
Ultimate Dream

Journey Stop
One

Experiencing the Gifts
of the Journey

I'm not afraid to die. I'm afraid of not living—not living my life according to God's plan for me, His plan for me as a parent. Proverbs 22:6 says to "train up a child in the way he should go." These words whispered to my heart as our family began this special journey.

Late in the fall of 2006, I leaned against the convention center wall in our hometown, waiting for my daughter Kenzie to be interviewed by a local television station. I overheard the conversation between the anchor and Kenzie.

"Why do you like Carrie Underwood so much?"

"Well," Kenzie replied, "she gave me the gift of dreams."

I smiled. What insight from such a young child. I never thought of dreams as being a gift until my daughter's words rang in my ears. Later that week, I still pondered that experience—Kenzie comprehended the concept that someone could give her a gift of that nature. That moment was another "aha" moment for me—little did I know it would impact my life in more ways than one.

A day or two had passed after Kenzie's interview, and I was Christmas shopping. I found myself standing in the electronics department surrounded by items my children already owned. *What am I going to buy them that they don't already have?* Emptiness swept over me—I felt lost with nothing new to give them.

Christmas came and went. The school year rolled along as usual. Everything in life was routine. But this haunting realization of emptiness in our lives wouldn't go away. It bothered me daily, and I prayed for a solution. I wanted to give my children something significant—gifts that only time and love could buy.

I can't really remember when I got so busy that I forgot the true meaning of a gift. Sometime in the last ten years, between play dates, sporting events, parties, school functions, and being homeroom mom, I got lost in the pursuit of material possessions. I went through the motions like so many of us do. I can remember when my kids smiled for the first time, and what a gift that was. And when I took Luke for well-baby checkups, I returned home happy that he had gained an ounce or two. As an enthusiastic, doting mother, I found myself showering my kids with *stuff*, never realizing the harm. As parents, we all experience the desire to give our children good gifts. Yet the gifts I consistently doled out to my children desensitized them to the true gifts—the lasting gifts that impact others and us for life.

As a stay-at-home mom, I had fallen into the trap of thinking the latest gadget was a necessity for my children. My kids had to have the coolest things on the market, and I delighted in providing them. I provided those temporal things not at their request, but just because *I could*. I was caught up in instant gratification, not for them but *for me*. My daughter's words during that interview brought to my attention the meaning of a transcendent gift—the *gift of dreams*.

That moment—leaning against the wall at the convention center and listening to the interview—I began to come to grips with the true meaning of a gift. Certainly, I knew that the two greatest gifts in life arrived in the form of Kenzie and Luke: my gifts from God. I know now that because they are gifts from God, I need to teach them the meaning and significance of true, lasting gifts.

During this time of reflection, I realized my children didn't recognize the gifts already filling their world, and I had created this dulled understanding. So how was I going to get back on God's path for me as a parent, leading and teaching them about God's gifts for them that are free and full of love? Sure, Kenzie recognized the gift of dreams, but did she understand how many gift-givers filled her life every single day? We went to church every Sunday, yet my daughter didn't recognize the gifts of greatness surrounding her. I was convinced I had done this to her, so I was determined to change the situation.

The turning point came when Kenzie approached me one night and showed me a magazine interview featuring Carrie Underwood. One of the questions, "What was the last book you read?" led to Carrie's answer, "*The Ultimate Gift.*"

Kenzie wanted to go purchase the book immediately. So we did. We began reading it that night. Little did I know that this was my answered prayer and the introduction to the gifts that only time and love could buy. This book would begin a gift-giving journey for our entire family.

I realized that I could take my children on this journey, and along the way, I could show them they are surrounded by gifts every day of their lives and that many of those gifts are free. I envisioned leading them to that place of greatness, where the things that matter are lasting, eternal. I purposed to lead them on a gift-giving journey, where the ultimate gift comes in understanding and accepting Jesus Christ.

At that point, I knew I wanted to take my children on a journey where I would give them a sequence of gifts that would impact their lives forever. After reading *The Ultimate Gift*, I knew I could become a true gift-giver to my children. It happened that fast for me. It was like reading a story about our lives, and I didn't want my kids to play the roles I had assigned to them. I had to change the script now.

I would've loved to give both my children this gift at the same time, but because of Luke's age and the fact that Kenzie was old enough to understand a journey of this magnitude, I decided it was the perfect time to focus on Kenzie. She was asking questions about baptism, and so it seemed like the perfect opportunity to introduce her to this journey—a journey leading to character growth and maturity through the gifts God provides. I began to pray for God to open doors leading to great opportunities for Kenzie to learn about the gift-givers in her life.

In the beginning, I searched for people everyone would recognize—entertainers, media spokespeople, corporate executives, and other famous faces. I was blessed along this journey to speak to Mr. Stovall, the author of *The Ultimate Gift*. At various stages of our journey, he offered priceless advice, a great gift itself.

One afternoon while sitting in his office, he challenged me to rethink my vision of the journey. "Heather, Kenzie is surrounded by ordinary gift-givers who give in extraordinary ways every single day. Don't be distracted by fame."

I love reality checks.

So I searched our community for people who are givers in their everyday walk. For twelve weeks,

I called strangers and friends alike, and I attended meetings with many "ordinary" people accomplishing extraordinary tasks and getting little recognition. I found along the way that I hadn't been aware of the many unselfish individuals in my own little world. In those twelve weeks, this mother of two went on her own journey and learned about the gifts in our family's life. The challenge came in making the decision to seek and find them. In those three months, I discovered many sacrificial people who wanted to make an impact on my daughter's life. In so doing, they impacted my entire family and me as well. As I walked the streets to find gift-givers, I found new friends. For the first time in my life I was really seeing the gifts in our world and the opportunities to be a gift-giver.

With every door that shut, another door opened, and that opportunity or experience proved better than the original plan. Soon this journey was not only touching Kenzie and me, but it also began to affect those who shared our journey and bystanders who heard about our experiences. It was contagious.

Each day, I shared with my husband Doug about the events that transpired and the people who crossed my path. They all had their own stories or their own reasons for wanting to be a part of our journey. Each and every individual made an impact and became an intricate part of our experience.

Doug and I decided on seven different gifts for the journey. If God could make the world in seven days, then we could show Kenzie seven different ways that she receives gifts from God. We decided to give Kenzie the gifts of *giving, learning, family, work, friends,* and *dreams,* and more than anything else, we wanted her to experience the *ultimate gift* of a relationship with Jesus Christ. This whole concept of giving Kenzie a journey started with one idea in mind—to help her understand that the ultimate gift of Jesus Christ was more priceless than any other gift she could ever receive.

Our family went to the lake with friends to celebrate this journey that lay ahead of us. It was more of a celebration and time of reflection for Doug and me, because Kenzie still knew nothing about this journey that would begin in less than seventy-two hours. On the way home, I had another "aha" moment, one of many yet to come. I was driving while Doug was in the backseat with the kids watching a movie. The quiet ride provided some time for soul-searching. I was praying that God would give me a sign that this journey was right for my daughter. At that moment, I saw a beautiful sunset and pointed it out to my family. As we witnessed the splendor of the moment, my eyes fell on an inscription in the rocks on a small hill: Jesus. I was overwhelmed with emotion and humbled by the message. It was like receiving a text message from God. I've never been as sure of anything in my life as I was at that moment. Now, armed with bundles of faith, I prayed. *Thank you, Lord. Let the journey begin.*

Journey Stop
Two

The Gift of Giving

I t's time for the big surprise." I looked at Kenzie as she sat with two of our friends; Joanne and Susan are like adopted mothers to me. They've been a great support system for me through the years. Since neither my mom nor Doug could be at the church for this big day, Joanne and Susan were fill-in family.

Kenzie and I arrived at our church that morning and found the meeting room set up just as I had previously arranged. The television screen was blue, waiting for the video to begin. A red box with a green bow sat in the middle of the round table, and a Bible was open next to it.

"Kenzie, over the past twelve weeks, we've planned a gift-giving journey for you. This six-week journey consists of a number of gifts from different gift-givers. You'll receive many of these gifts by video, and then you will be challenged to go out and experience them. I want you to have the time of your life this summer and enjoy this journey."

I then turned to Kenzie and kissed her on the cheek and finished by saying, "I love you very much. Are you ready to receive your first gift?"

I hit play on the video player, and the face of a seventy-six-year-old woman appeared on the screen.

"Kenzie, my name is Anne. I've worked for Meals On Wheels for the last ten years and volunteered for them for several more. I've always liked the feeling I get when I give to others. This week you will receive the *gift of giving.* You'll make one hundred handmade cards. Then you will be challenged to go and deliver them with the meals we take to people in need. I'm also challenging you to give away some of your most treasured bears to an area shelter or charity of your choice. Report back to the church when this gift is completed to receive your next gift."

I turned on the lights only to find tears in Kenzie's eyes.

"Honey, what's wrong?"

"I am just so happy." My daughter was happy that I had taken the time to plan such an event and journey just for her. The love in the room was overwhelming.

As the tears flowed, so did the excitement of what this journey was to hold.

"Mom, what's in the box?"

I scooted the red box over to her. She opened the box. Inside, she found everything she needed to make her cards.

As we prayed, another friend entered the room. Don had also been invited to the meeting and knew Kenzie from church. He assured Kenzie that if she needed any support along the way, many people were available to help her.

When we got in the car, Kenzie began decorating a card in her excitement to begin this journey. Kenzie spoke with her father on the phone, and I could hear the excitement in her voice as she shared with her daddy the news of the gift she had received. We had three days to make the cards before the meal deliveries would take place. I became concerned after she had finished about forty of the cards. Kenzie began to slow down, and I realized this was a big challenge.

When I asked if I could help, she responded, "Mom, this is my gift and my chance to learn, not yours." As hard as that was to hear, I was thankful. It showed me she possessed the determination needed to accomplish this gift on her own—another lesson for mom.

I listened and watched as Kenzie explained to everyone who came by our home the reason behind the cards and how excited she was to share them with others. After hours of making each and every card unique, we left to begin the deliveries with Anne.

On our way, Kenzie and I talked about the meaning behind this journey.

I explained that I wanted her to meet people who make a difference every day, like Anne with Meals On Wheels. Kenzie now had the opportunity to make a difference in many lives. I recalled when I first met Anne on the phone.

"Meals On Wheels, this is Anne speaking. May I help you?"

I explained the purpose of my call—to set up the *gift of giving* experience for my daughter Kenzie. When I stepped in the Meals On Wheels office a few days later, I knew immediately who Anne was—the nice lady with a warm voice. I felt as if I had known her my whole life. I watched her answer the phone a few times while I was there, and she displayed the same friendly, helpful attitude with everyone who called: "No ma'am, we have you on the schedule for Wednesday. Are you feeling good today? Yes, ma'am, we will be there. Have a good day."

I explained to Kenzie how I learned about Anne's dedication to Meals On Wheels when I originally filmed her. She gave years to the organization; she was committed to deliver meals and good cheer, year after year, as well as answer phones and help around the office. Anne blessed others by giving of herself. I was humbled to have her as one of Kenzie's gift-givers on the journey.

When Kenzie asked me why I spent so much time getting this ready for her, I responded that she and her brother were the two most priceless gifts I'd ever been given. I wanted to teach her about the gifts she can receive every day, explaining that the sooner she understood them, the sooner she would also be blessed by them. She was excited about being able to help others and give of herself.

"Mom, do you think Ms. Anne will like me?" Kenzie asked as we arrived at the Meals On Wheels office the day of her gift-giving experience. As she asked, we heard a friendly voice in the kitchen—Anne. Kenzie smiled, realizing her question had been answered. She knew she would enjoy this new relationship.

"Well, there you are, Kenzie." Anne embraced Kenzie in a grandmotherly hug and gave her a hat to wear for the day. Kenzie showed Anne the cards she made to hand out with each delivery.

"I'm so proud of you, Kenzie, for taking the time to create these special cards. These will make our friends so happy." Anne hugged Kenzie again before we got to work.

We loaded coolers in Anne's car. Kenzie sat in the front as Anne's helper. While Anne drove, she explained the service provided by Meals On Wheels and how it impacts those it serves.

"Kenzie, we bless many people every day."

As we delivered meals that day, Kenzie encountered many inspiring individuals, and they all had a story to share. Many talked about giving, and some were just excited to have someone to talk to. It was hard for me as a mother not to be the director that day, but I sat back and watched my daughter share her story with others and learn along the way.

One woman told Kenzie that the most important lesson of her ninety-three years of living was learning to treat others as she wanted to be treated—the Golden Rule. Such a simple lesson, one that I'd told my children time and time again, but in that moment it impacted Kenzie more than any of my previous lectures. Kenzie fell into this woman's arms and hugged her tightly. She wanted to talk to her longer, but we had many more people to feed.

During another stop, we met a lonely, frail woman who seemed happy to see a child's face. The lady shared with us that she was excited to have moved into a two-room apartment with air conditioning. *Air conditioning.* Something we all take for granted. I notice the puzzled look on Kenzie's face when we walked to the car.

"Doesn't everyone have air conditioning?" Kenzie asked.

Anne and I explained that many people live without the conveniences that we are so fortunate to have. Kenzie seemed shocked. After some quiet moments, Kenzie's concerns came out as she talked about hugs being free and how we are all capable of giving those. I was beginning to see a change in my daughter. Her perspective of the world was widening. She was having fun as a gift-giver, and others were blessing her. The journey had only begun, but already we were both impacted.

Out of the eight stops that day, number seven changed my daughter's view of the word "giving." Kenzie stood on the front porch. The man opened the door slowly. He had a smile from ear to ear in spite of the oxygen tank that followed him.

"I'm delivering your meal today because I'm on a special journey. I'm experiencing the gift of giving," Kenzie explained to the man.

"I know all about that particular gift. I have the heart of a sixteen-year-old beating in my chest because another family valued the gift of giving, even though they were enduring terrible loss when they made the decision to give." The man continued to smile. "They understood what it meant to give."

"You have the heart of a sixteen-year-old?" Kenzie asked.

"Yes, I received a heart transplant a few months ago. I need the heart to live, but my relationship with the donor family is the greatest gift I received. I've been given a second chance not only to be alive, but also to be a part of someone's family."

Devastating loss didn't stop the donor family from thinking about someone else's need. They saw through their pain—the death of their teenage son— and realized they could make a difference, even in horrible tragedy. They knew what it meant to give.

The man at stop seven knew what it cost to live. He understood the price the donor family had paid in order for him to take another breath. He valued them—he recognized that human relationships were more precious than the breath of life itself. Physical existence didn't compare to the connection he had with other people. This man understood what mattered most.

While he was sharing his story, I wrapped my arms around Kenzie for support. She in return held me close as her eyes filled with tears. I looked at Kenzie and asked her, "Honey, isn't that a cool gift of giving?"

"One of the best, Mom."

I shook his hand and thanked him for blessing us; he helped show my daughter the gift of giving.

Kenzie's gift that day came from what she received and learned, as well as the gifts she gave. Making and giving away handmade cards, giving her time by listening, sharing a hug and a warm hello, and delivering meals taught my daughter about giving in ways that words could never teach.

Kenzie learned that giving oneself in the form of physical labor is a gift—a service from the heart that blesses others. She witnessed Anne giving wholeheartedly and demonstrating that serving others blesses them and honors God.

With each delivery, the recipients thanked Anne enthusiastically and carried on warm conversations—it was obvious they looked forward to more than a meal. The friendship they experienced with Anne extended beyond the boundaries of someone doing a mundane delivery or required duty. Anne put her heart into her work, and it showed. She was a blessing to everyone she came in contact with. We were blessed to witness her wholehearted devotion to others. Kenzie saw Anne put into practice that familiar Bible verse, "Whatever you do, do it all to the glory of God."

When we got home, Kenzie was anxious to complete the rest of the gift. She started going through her most beloved stuffed bears. At first, she was upset about having to make the decision about which ones to give away—they were all special and had been an important part of her life. But thinking about her day of giving inspired her to see this task differently. They were, after all, just bears—not air conditioning or a heart. She had many bears, she reasoned. Kenzie made a big pile of bears, giving each one a hug before she placed them in the give-away bag. She made the decision on her own to give away ten bears to an organization that makes bear bags for children when they experience a death in their family.

We took the bears to the church, and she again hugged each one before parting with them. She told the woman in charge of the Bear Bag Ministry that she was okay with giving them away, because she had a friend who had received a bag with a bear in it when she lost one of her family members. That friend sleeps with her bear every night. Kenzie knew the bears would be used to help someone else. They would be loved. I was proud of her that day, for on that day I knew Kenzie truly understood the gift of giving.

Journey Stop
Three

The Gift of Learning

Mom, do you think everyone who comes through these church doors receives gifts like mine?"

"I hope so. There's something for everyone here, if they'll just receive it."

We were seated at the table, and it was time for the next gift. Our eyes were glued to the screen as we watched an image appear on the screen—a woman sitting on a porch swing. When she began to speak, Kenzie recognized her.

"That's my principal!"

"Kenzie, I hope you're having a great time on this gift-giving journey. This week you'll experience the *gift of learning*. I've had the honor of being your principal for six years, and you're getting ready to enter the fourth grade. In twenty years as a principal, it's been a gift to see children excel every year on their journeys in life. Your challenge is to live out this gift of learning—you'll go to a host church for Project Transformation, a Christian organization providing community-oriented programs to children and youth from low-income neighborhoods. The children attend for eight weeks. You'll spend time with these children and participate in activities with them throughout the day. Another part of this challenge is to learn the importance of Scripture. Kenzie, you can always count on guidance in Scripture. The Bible provides direction for any situation in life—it's the perfect playbook. Have fun on this journey, and I look forward to talking with you about what you learn from this gift."

The television went blue, and we prayed. We thanked God for the opportunity to learn and receive this gift. Before we made the trip to Project Transformation, we spent a few days discussing and reviewing Bible verses applicable to this new challenge. As a family, we discussed different aspects of the journey, sharing stories and laughing together. Luke got involved alongside his sister, asking questions and learning.

As we reminisced together, I shared that while growing up, my favorite verse was Philippians 4:13—

"I can do all things through Christ who strengtheneth me." It helped me to approach the challenges of basketball. Kenzie's favorite scripture was John 3:16—"For God so loved the world, that He gave His only begotten son, that whosoever believeth in Him should not perish, but have everlasting life." It was amazing to watch how this journey was bringing the whole family together and touching each and every one of us in a different way.

The day arrived for the gift of learning. On the way, I said, "Kenzie, I realize you're just a child, but take this opportunity to learn to teach others. Everyone has something to teach or learn, no matter what the age."

Kenzie walked into Project Transformation ready to help other children learn. We were greeted by the sound of children involved in a variety of activities as Mr. Daniel led us to Kenzie's post. As Kenzie joined a group of a dozen children, she soon forgot her shyness and began reaching out to them.

Children naturally gravitate to other kids they like—maybe kids who look like them, laugh at the same jokes, or like the same games and toys. Kenzie was drawn to one little girl in particular, Allie, and they laughed and played together most of the day. Kenzie confided in me that she wanted to be Allie's partner during the literacy activity.

The activities built skills in computers, art, music, exercise, and literacy—an area where Kenzie excels. Reading has always come easily for Kenzie, so she was in familiar territory. She thought teaching Allie to read was her next new encounter.

But God had another plan. Another little girl in the class had zeroed in on Kenzie. Hope, a young girl with attention difficulties and who had trouble fitting in with the other children, had already approached the director of the literacy activity.

"I want to be with them." She picked us.

So Kenzie and I were paired with Hope. This helped Kenzie to grow. She put her own wishes aside and invested herself in this girl. Kenzie tried to help her and coax her along in her reading. It was apparent that Hope had trouble focusing, staying on task, and comprehending. Even with one-on-one attention, she was distracted throughout most of the activity. I observed with admiration as my daughter intuitively knew how to get this girl's attention. I wanted to intervene, but I stopped myself—this was Kenzie's gift, not mine. Instead of trying to smooth the process for Kenzie, I sat back and watched in awe.

Kenzie took Hope's hand and walked her to the bookshelf; she let Hope choose a book. We sat on the couch and read the book together. By the end of our time together, Kenzie and Hope were sitting side by side and learning together. Kenzie learned she could do something hard—and she liked the way she felt when she met the challenge with willingness. My daughter learned that she is capable of teaching another child, while the child she was teaching learned that other children want to help her. Another lesson learned for this mother of two—let go and let God work in the lives of our children.

Kenzie's original plan was to help a child she liked—a child who was more like her and her friends. But God had another plan, a plan to teach Kenzie to stretch and grow, to reach beyond her comfort zone to someone in need—someone who said, "I want to be with you." And Kenzie learned that opportunities don't always look easy or comfortable or familiar. Sometimes they come in the form of a "Hope" who may offer us very little at first glance, but when we look a little closer, we learn that we grow as we meet needs in others' lives. Both of them grew through the process. Kenzie walked into Project Transformation thinking she would help others learn, but Kenzie learned as well. That *gift of learning* experience taught Kenzie a valuable lesson—God has better plans.

Kenzie went on a treasure hunt with the older children that afternoon. She eagerly set out with her camera to capture the beauty of her world. The entire class was equipped with cameras and a mission: to take pictures of anything interesting or beautiful. But on this day and for this mission, Kenzie had eyes to see the treasures that surround her. I was also challenged to look for treasures in the ordinary things. The treasures they gathered were the ordinary things we passed on a daily basis a million times. I trailed behind and noticed Kenzie taking pictures of flowers, animals, clouds, trees, children, leaves, and houses and laughing the whole way. She turned to me a couple of times and said, "Isn't this fun, Mom?"—my wake-up call to see life differently, to look for treasures in everyday life.

As they saw life through the lens of a camera, I saw life through the eyes of a child. We have a great canvas that we live on called Earth. Our home is God's masterpiece.

I later developed the pictures. They look like postcards, they're so beautiful. One of my favorite moments that day was the time Kenzie stopped in the middle of the street and took a picture of the sky through two overgrown trees. She looked back at me with a smile and said, "Just took a little picture of Heaven."

Moms can set the stage for their children to become treasure hunters. Instead of hurrying our children from one activity to another and cramming the latest entertainment events into our children's crowded lives, we can teach them to slow down and wonder, to see the world with eyes trained to look for beauty in ordinary moments. We can teach our children that we are blessed as we develop eyes to see the beauty in ordinary, daily activities and things: clouds, trees, birds, and flowers, but most of all the blessings from God. We can give our children the gift of ordinary moments and unleash them to become treasure hunters.

"Are you coming back next week?" the children asked Kenzie as we said our good-byes.

"No, I'm sorry. I have another gift to receive on my gift-giving journey. I won't be able to join you next week." The children exchanged hugs with Kenzie as we left, and on the way home, Kenzie's conversation meandered over the highlights of the day.

"Mom, one of the girls told me she doesn't live with her mother anymore because her mom doesn't have time for her."

"I guess that's why God gave us other people in our lives."

"I'm so blessed to have my family—you, Dad, and Luke. I love you, Mom!"

"I love you, too." The day was worth every minute.

I gathered my thoughts as we drove home that day and was thankful for the opportunity to watch my daughter from afar and to be a part of an incredible experience with her. What a great gift.

As I tucked her into bed that night, I kissed her on the forehead and reminded her again of how very proud I was of her. Walking quietly to my room, I thought about how those were the moments I would treasure forever.

A couple of days passed, and Kenzie and I reviewed her Bible verses to complete her experience with the *gift of learning.* We talked about how the Bible can be a playbook for our lives, how we can turn to it in any situation we encounter. She repeated her favorite verse, the first one she ever learned, John 3:16. I reminded her that the Bible is full of many truths to learn, but John 3:16 is where it all begins—that God gave His only Son for us to have eternal life. And as Kenzie experienced the gift of learning, she was reminded that the ultimate gift-giver—God—gave it all.

Journey Stop
Four

The Gift of Family

A week passed, and we were excited about going on vacation as a family. I didn't really know how I was going to fit the *gift of family* in our busy lives, but throughout this journey, I was learning that God has His own timing. Everything works out in His time frame, and there's always a reason for every encounter we face.

We had loaded the car and were headed for the airport when the question came up.

"Mom, when am I going to receive my next gift?" Kenzie was getting into this gift-giving journey. Luke chimed in, so I touched the play button on the car DVD player.

The video screen lit up, and Kenzie immediately recognized the participants in the next gift, the *gift of family*. The faces of three generations appeared, and Kenzie listened to her great-grandmother; her grandmother, Grammie; her great-aunt; and her mother share the impact that family has had on each one of them.

"I grew up in a two-bedroom home—and we had seven in our family."

"We didn't get toys like you do—I remember when I got my bike. Only one of us got a bike that year."

"Family is a blessing—treat each family member as a gift."

"We may not always agree, but we also have a gift in the freedom to disagree lovingly."

"Pray hard and live life to the fullest."

We each shared words of advice, along with tender moments of loving and losing family members. My aunt's daughter, Julie, had passed away years earlier, and my aunt shared the pain of that loss, along with the blessing of the daughter she had loved. Julie was Kenzie's namesake.

I ended the video clip with a challenge: "Kenzie, you'll see your grandparents when the plane lands in California, but look around—God will show you different definitions of family throughout your trip."

Kenzie's grandparents met us at the airport and took us to our hotel room, where Kenzie was delighted to discover our room number to be her favorite Bible verse address—316. This would be a wonderful start not only to a vacation but also to one of the most memorable journey moments. What a beginning to this experience of the gift of family!

As Kenzie experienced the gift of family, I marveled that three generations had shared in our journey. I recognized the value in the presence of these loved ones—Kenzie's great-grandmother, grandmother, and great-aunt. The wisdom these women had garnered through the years was a treasure. The love they poured out was a gift. We experienced the blessing of family as we made that journey stop.

When we've cried by the graveside of someone dear, the pain compels us to examine how deeply we value those still in our lives. We know that tomorrow may be too late. We learn to cherish the moments of being together and belonging. Death teaches us to live with appreciation for those around us today.

This journey would help us to cherish family members as gifts, to value every moment we have together, to see the blessing in each individual, and to treat them as gifts, whether we are related or not.

Kenzie and I walked the beach early the next morning. We witnessed lines of homeless people next to the seawall, sheltered by only blankets. Empty shopping carts dotted the scene.

"Mom, why are they out here?"

"They probably think they have nowhere else to go."

"But they all have God. He's here for everyone."

I was starting to see that throughout this journey, Kenzie had developed an understanding about the gifts around her. Our journey was weaving a tapestry in my young daughter's soul.

As we made our way to the nearby pier, Kenzie's eyes landed on a tent pitched near the California ocean waves. In big, bold letters, a "JOHN 3:16" banner appeared on the side.

Kenzie and I both felt the significance of that moment—that God had delivered a message on the beach, and we knew we were following God's footprints in the sand. *Thanks, Lord, for being here.* My heart felt gratitude that God was present on our journey.

We approached the tent, and there was a man standing beside it.

"Are you having church?" Kenzie asked.

"Yes, we are. Would you like to come?" Pastor Rick responded.

"Why are you here so early?" Kenzie asked.

"Well, this is when the brokenhearted come."

Pastor Rick was on the beach every Sunday morning, reaching out to others and sharing the gifts of God with those who came. Pastor Rick was available. It probably wasn't the most convenient time for him, but it was the moment of someone else's need. He didn't let his personal preferences limit his ministry.

That morning, Pastor Rick offered Kenzie and others on the beach the gift of extended family, and we witnessed the beauty of another gift-giver along our journey.

Pastor Rick was an example of selfless giving, and Kenzie and I both learned from him. Kenzie felt comfortable enough with him to share about her gift-giving journey and that she had received the gift of eternal life through Jesus Christ.

Our last day in California arrived, and our whole family was on the beach that morning. I arranged our chairs next to a man lying on a blanket surrounded by only a few items. His name was William.

"Are you from this area or just visiting?" William struck up a conversation.

Normally, I would've been cautious about carrying on a conversation with a stranger on the beach, but we weren't alone, and I had learned a lot that week about the homeless. I shared with him about our journey, and I asked him if he wouldn't mind sharing about his life's journey with Kenzie.

"I hear you're on a special journey," William began when Kenzie joined us.

"Yes, this week I received the *gift of family*, and we are celebrating ours."

"Kenzie, Mr. William lives here on this beach—it's his home," I said.

"Are you scared?" Kenzie looked on wide-eyed as she listened to William's story.

"No, and you shouldn't be either. I've got a daughter your mother's age, and I go see her once a month. I pick up cans and earn money by working. I've got a wallet and a bank account just like your mom and dad. What do you think is the most important thing I have out here?"

"A Bible."

"You're right about the Bible, but I was thinking about a bike. That's how I get around."

William picked up his Bible. "I spend a lot of time with God out here. I probably won't be here much longer, but I needed some time to sort out my life." He took his time explaining life from his perspective, and my children learned that even others who live differently have something to offer.

Kenzie learned how someone could be content with the beach as his home and only a few possessions—just enough to fit into a small black bag. William's view of family stretched Kenzie's understanding of the word.

"Family isn't always those you are related to. Lots of people look after me."

"Pastor Rick holds church on the beach every Sunday morning—the people who go to his tent could be part of your family too." Kenzie was eager for William to have a church family.

As we packed to return home, Kenzie surprised me with an announcement.

"I want to leave our boogie boards and drinks with William. Maybe he can sell them and earn some extra money."

"Me too," Luke chimed in. The giving was contagious.

We had introduced our children to many gifts by sharing our time with a man who was homeless but full of hope. Our children also learned that family is often given to us not only by birth, but also by choice.

As we delivered the items to William, we saw tears in his eyes. Kenzie and Luke wanted a picture to remember him and his story. As Doug and I walked down the beach with them, I was amazed that my children had wanted to sit by a homeless man on a blanket and have their picture taken. They wrapped their arms around him as if they were leaving one of their family members for the weekend. How far we had come. *Eyes wide open, Lord. Thank you for insight into life as it is, for not only my children but also myself. It brings light and a reminder to my soul of the truth I was brought up with—the Lord shows up when we least expect it and in ways we can't always anticipate. Thank you, Lord, for not only teaching my children to be humble, but for humbling my soul also.*

On the way home, my kids wanted reassurance that William would be okay.

"He'll be fine. He told me he is saved—he believes in Jesus. He knows that he's surrounded by gift-givers who help him, and he's content," I assured them. "William said lots of people look after him."

But I wondered as we made our trip to the airport, how many Williams out there have no one looking after them?

Maybe you wonder too. Who do you look after? Are you willing to be inconvenienced by an elderly individual, a mentally or physically disabled person, or an ill or homeless person? Do you even notice the man who struggles to get his wheelchair around a tight corner or the elderly person who can't reach an item on a high shelf in the store? Have you contributed or volunteered at your local food bank or even had a simple conversation with a homeless man? Are you willing to offer a job to someone who's out of work? Who do you look after? Where's your William?

We boarded the plane much richer than when we arrived in California. Our understanding of the gift of family had grown, and we were different. Who could've imagined that a homeless man on the beach could have enriched our lives and opened our eyes to see the true gift of family?

Journey Stop
Five

The Gift of Work

D o we have to do this?" Kenzie became bored quickly with her new gift experience—the *gift of work*. Sorting school supplies and cleaning the supply room of the food bank in Tahlequah lost the appeal of the gift experience, but only for a short while.

"This is work, Kenzie. Most people work for a living, and some people work for free." I wanted Kenzie to understand the gift of volunteering as well as the gift of work.

"They give the gift of work for free?"

"Yes, we're doing it right now—volunteering our time to help without getting paid."

I explained to Kenzie that without volunteers and their "free" work, many people would never receive the help they need.

Ms. Kate had introduced Kenzie to this gift on the video screen during the drive into Tahlequah. "I'm the head of volunteer services for the food bank in our city. This week, you will receive the *gift of work*. Our organization needs the help of many people in order to run. I always like the feeling I get when I give to others. You will be challenged to live out this gift by volunteering at the Cookson Hills Ministry. You will be handing out school supplies, helping clean vans, organizing supplies and storerooms, and cleaning. If you have time, you'll also come to the food bank and help sort and box canned goods."

On the way to the ministry building, I explained to Kenzie how the food bank worked. I told her they fed about fifty thousand people a week and that one-fifth of them were children. Kenzie seemed shocked that there were actually children who didn't eat every day. I saw her become very concerned about this problem, and she asked me how we could help.

Kenzie arrived at her mission site eager to begin.

The woman who greeted us, Ms. Debbie, explained that many children in the area couldn't afford school supplies or backpacks, so the ministry provided those items. As our guide explained Kenzie's jobs for the day, another young boy walked in—also to help. He was given job assignments, and he quickly got to work.

Kenzie waited for her first recipients to walk through the door. She waited and waited. No one came for a while, so Ms. Debbie gave Kenzie the jobs of refilling school supplies and straightening the supply room. This is the point the glitter of the gift of work was lost on Kenzie and boredom set in.

After our discussion about work and volunteerism, Kenzie and I cut soup labels. Kenzie became tired quickly, but she became energized when her first family walked in for school supplies. Kenzie carefully selected the colors of Kleenex boxes and school boxes to "match" the gender of the child—she wanted them to be happy. The boredom of the gift of work evaporated when Kenzie began to take an interest in each individual she served, when she interacted with the real people whose lives she was touching.

Ms. Debbie took us on a tour of the ministry facilities after Kenzie handed out supplies. As we walked through the thrift store, Kenzie realized that a trip to the mall wasn't every kid's experience. Some kids got their "new" clothes here, and they weren't new at all—they were someone else's hand-me-downs. Kenzie understood that she had clothes in her closet, as well as her hamper, that would help others.

"Did you know that some children don't have food to eat over the weekends?" Ms. Debbie asked Kenzie as we walked into the food donation building. "That's why we send food home with the children when they leave school on Fridays."

"How can we change that?" my daughter asked. She was beginning to understand that she could make a difference in other children's lives. She was also thankful for what she had.

We ate lunch at the Senior Citizens Building, and then we moved boxes of donated clothing.

By the end of the day, Kenzie possessed a better understanding of volunteerism and the gift of work—she even grasped the significance of the work her father and I do. She realized work is something anyone can give to others, and she certainly had a better appreciation for those who volunteer—definitely gift-givers.

A few days later, Kenzie shared a wider perspective of this gift of work.

"You know, all the gifts have some sort of work involved." The handmade cards that she made were work. Organizing the gift experiences for others was work. Helping the kids at the camp was work, no matter what they needed.

She was right. Every experience involved giving of herself and reaching out to others. This was a form of work—an act of service. There was finally a sudden awareness that no matter what you do, there is work involved, whether you volunteer or get paid.

Kenzie is more aware of helping others, even at home. She looks for opportunities to help. Because of this awareness of Kenzie and the gift of work, Luke now wants to give of himself, even if it's just cleaning his own room. Watching all of the volunteers and the selfless people working in the nonprofit organizations has impressed upon me the importance of teaching my children to give back what they receive. Work, no matter what type, will always be work, but the benefit is in the attitude we have as we work.

I also want my kids to understand that volunteers know the blessing of giving. Kids learn quickly how to say "mine." They're born with a natural bent to choose the best for themselves—the biggest brownie on the plate, the best seat at the movie, the to-the-top-full cup of soda at the table. Kids naturally know how to claim the most desirable toy at group playtime. As they grow, they're also well skilled at avoiding the dishes when Mom calls out for a helper, and they have a knack for disappearing when the laundry needs to be folded. Forget about the possibility of their noticing that the trash is overflowing.

Serving others at the expense of our personal comfort isn't an innate trait for most humans. It's learned. Kids and adults alike learn the pleasure of serving others by becoming involved in the lives of those with needs. When we see others experiencing difficult circumstances or living with few material goods and we have the opportunity to make life a little better for those who struggle, we experience a blessing. We are changed. We learn that giving the best to others can bless us beyond any material payoff—we learn the blessing of volunteering, the blessing of giving of ourselves.

Since she has experienced this gift, I think Kenzie understands. I heard her say to a friend the other day, "Somehow or someway, you will help someone by giving the gift of work."

Journey Stop
Six

The Gift of Friends

C an I borrow your kids for the weekend?"
The next gift-giving experience for Kenzie involved
neighborhood kids and a weekend sleepover: the *gift
of friends.*

My friend Angie had followed our journey and
welcomed the idea of letting her kids in on the
adventure. I announced to Kenzie, Luke, Jordan, and
Alex that they all were a part of the next gift, and then
I started the video.

"Hi, guys, it's just me. Over the last few months, Kenzie has received different gifts and faced the challenge to live those out. Kenzie has received the gifts of *giving, learning, family,* and *work.* We wanted to show Kenzie that she is surrounded by gift-givers every day of her life and that God finds opportunities to use them. Today we are giving Kenzie the *gift of friends.* Kenzie, you have always said that Jordan is one of your best friends, and Alex and Luke are great friends also. We want you to learn to consider friendship as a gift. We're going to Grammie and Papa's house for the weekend, and we'll celebrate friendship. You can swim all day and stay up as late as you want, as long as you realize why we are going.

"Jordan and Alex, I consider your mom one of my great friends. We may not agree on everything all the time, but I feel as if I can call her in any situation and she'll be there. We've never lived around many family members, but friends have substituted in many situations. Whether it's Grandparents' Day, the book fair, or church, God has always provided me with a friend to stand in.

"In high school, I had a basketball coach named Sherri. She was a great leader for others and me. We've stayed in touch through all these years. God placed us together to travel this journey as friends. God used her to coach me on this special journey with my daughter.

"Throughout your lives you will have many friends. Some will change as you grow up, but you'll also have those who stay in your life forever. Those friends are gifts from God—true friends."

We picked up Kenzie's cousin Mady the next morning on the way to their grandmother's house. The next two days were filled with singing and laughter, pool times and talk times. They played hockey, climbed into the tree house, rode bikes, and swam for hours.

On the way home, we realized how well they had all gotten along. I considered it a true gift that five children never fought during this adventure. We thanked God for the gift of friendship, a gift we can give or receive. Everyone needs friends.

Along this journey, I was struck by the realization of how my friends are blessings. We often take our friends for granted—how much we need them and how readily we depend on them. I wanted this experience to be a reminder for my kids that friendship is a gift; I also wanted my kids to remember anew the truth to the old saying: "To have a friend you must be a friend." We need to unwrap the gift of friendship inside of us and give it away—then, we can truly become a friend.

Kids seem to put this principle into practice better at earlier ages—they seem intuitively to know how to save a seat in the lunchroom for the child they want for a friend. They leave a Skittle on the desk of the kid they want to play with at recess, and they offer to let their friend ride their bike first when they come over to play. They cover up for friends when the teacher wants to know "who did it," and they defend their friends when parents question "who did it." Simple acts of kindness make a difference in the lives of others; they show we care, and more importantly, they show God cares. Acts of kindness don't take a significant amount of time, but they usually make a significant impact. Remember to take the time to be a friend and to teach your children how to be friends.

Children sometimes lose the ability to put others first as they grow into adulthood. Our culture often sends the message to "look out for number one" and "don't put up with anything."

While it's true that we want our children to be safe from predators and to discern inappropriate demands and expectations from others, we also need to instill a genuine concern for the welfare of others. Sometimes that costs us. The cost may be in the form of time, money, or energy, but the blessing of being used by God to touch someone else's life is worth the effort. Our kids need to experience the gift of being a friend.

That weekend, Kenzie wasn't the only one blessed by a gift. Jordan, Alex, Luke, and Mady also experienced the gift of friends.

Journey Stop
Seven

The Gift of Dreams

re you ready?" I heard my friend Sherri's voice. "Breathe!"

And I knew it was going to happen—Kenzie's biggest surprise so far.

"Tony Romo said your names were on the list for the meet and greet with Carrie Underwood. When you get to the will call window at the concert, you'll get your passes. Kenzie is now getting the *gift of dreams*."

I called my husband Doug and cried most of the way home. This gift had been in the works for months, and now we would see it come to fruition. In less than five hours, we would board a plane to fulfill Kenzie's dream.

The 2005 American Idol winner Carrie Underwood had been Kenzie's inspiration for the previous two years. Kenzie followed this extraordinary hero on her journey to stardom. Kenzie's fascination with Carrie Underwood had remained steadfast; the inspiration Carrie provided for her followers was enduring. Kenzie now believes dreams can come true because of Carrie Underwood.

Kenzie also admired Carrie for her willingness to give God the credit for the good things in her life. My daughter watched Carrie during her American Idol tours, and Kenzie was inspired as Carrie publicly gave thanks to God for everything she had been given.

"Where's my lunch?" Kenzie asked as I approached her in the school cafeteria after getting the news from Sherri. Kenzie had no idea she was about to go on the biggest trip of her life.

"Why don't you come with me?"

Patti, the principal, had asked to be a part of the surprise, so we headed to her office. We passed a plaque on her wall bearing a message I had come to understand: "To the world you may be just one person, but to one person you may be the world."

"Kenzie, you've worked so hard on this journey. When people give to others, they receive blessings in return," Patti began. I jumped in.

"Kenzie, you'll get on a plane for Pennsylvania in less than an hour. You're going to meet Carrie Underwood."

Kenzie fell into my arms crying—her dream was coming true.

After the plane took off, I reflected on the journey. The work involved in preparing the experiences, the way details had been carefully attended to, how God had orchestrated circumstances to make everything work out better than I could imagine, how so many people had been involved in the process—behind the scenes as well as front and center on the video recordings. My husband Doug had worked out our travel arrangements for this gift with very little notice, but he was thrilled he could contribute in that way. I gave thanks to God for making everything fall into place—only a big God could make this happen.

The next morning, Kenzie's excitement bubbled. We had an entire day before the concert that evening, so we shopped and had our nails manicured. Mom and daughter time was filled with fun and anticipation for the upcoming night's events.

When we arrived at the concert, we spotted Carrie's bus. At the will call window, we ran into some problems. They didn't have the meet and greet list yet, so Kenzie and I walked around while Kenzie talked about what she wanted to say to Carrie. She also had a card prepared to give to her hero. I encouraged her to tell Carrie how she had impacted Kenzie's life— how Kenzie had learned to dream big by watching Carrie's life.

As we meandered through the fairgrounds, we heard Carrie's voice over the mike. They were doing a sound check. Kenzie ran toward the front gates and joined a line of fans hoping to catch a closer glimpse of their idol as she walked to her bus. Carrie came to them, pausing for pictures and brief exchanges with her fans. Carrie finally stood before Kenzie, and I saw Kenzie's chest heave in a deep breath.

"Hi, Carrie."

"Hi. Would you like a picture?" Carrie turned toward me, put her arm around Kenzie, and smiled. I snapped the picture. Carrie lingered a few moments before disappearing into her bus. Kenzie was walking on clouds, and it wasn't even time for the meet and greet.

When we approached the will call window again, they had the list. If we had our way, Kenzie would've been first in line to meet Carrie Underwood in the meet and greet. There we stood in Pennsylvania waiting to meet Kenzie's hero, but we faced one huge problem. Someone had left her name off the list, and it looked like Kenzie's dream was about to evaporate before our eyes.

We faced the possibility of not spending time with Carrie after flying to the concert from out of state. Kenzie collapsed into tears against the wall.

"You have to pull yourself together. This will work out, I promise. We'll leave Pennsylvania learning a great lesson, whatever that lesson is supposed to be." I didn't think to remind her that she had just met the object of her adoration, even though her name wasn't on the list. I knew we both wanted more time with Kenzie's hero, and we didn't want those brief moments of snapping a picture to be all we experienced of this dream. Kenzie dissolved into tears as I dialed my friend Sherri's number.

Sherri had been a gift-giver on this journey, and I especially needed her help and support in this moment.

"Heather, have faith everything will work out. Now look around you and see if anyone is affiliated with Carrie. The people with whom you are talking at the will call window work for the fair, not for Carrie. While you're looking, let me talk to Kenzie."

Sherri quickly took charge and offered consolation to my daughter as I stumbled off to find someone who could make this situation turn out right. I breathed a silent prayer for God to make this work out.

I took a chance on a man standing near Carrie's bus. He was the man who could help me. I had the passes in my hand when I approached Kenzie a few moments later. When I returned, Kenzie was talking calmly on the phone with Sherri.

"Kenzie's so calm now—what did you say to her?" I asked Sherri when I got the phone from my daughter.

"I told her to take a deep breath, pray, and believe everything will work out. Someday you'll again be in a similar situation and be scared that things are not going according to your plans. You have to believe that everything happens for a reason. That's faith. You've got to believe everything is in God's control."

In that moment, Sherri spoke to my heart as well as my daughter's. I needed to be reminded to breathe and have faith.

My daughter and I learned several important lessons that afternoon at the concert in York. The most important one—just have faith. Kenzie knew what faith was, but she experienced it firsthand that afternoon. She believed for over two years that someday this would happen, and it was hours away from coming true. However, we needed those moments of uncertainty to be reminded—just breathe and have faith. Believe that God cares about the details of our lives, and nothing is impossible with God.

But God has His own plan, and unfortunately, it doesn't always line up with our expectations. It may be a very different plan. In our case, He had a reason for a list, and a reason for a name being left off a list. Kenzie's name was missing, and because I had to scramble to fix the problem, Kenzie wasn't first in line. In fact, she was next to the last in line, where a child named Lauren stood behind her. And while we dreamed of meeting Carrie Underwood, God arranged for us to meet Lauren.

As we waited at the back of the line, some people from a wish-granting organization joined us. The wish foundation is a gift-giver in a big way—they make dreams come true for seriously ill children. The recipient of this wish was a little girl named Lauren, and she was receiving her wish to meet Carrie Underwood.

Kenzie's view of what was really important shifted during her conversation with Lauren. Kenzie realized that more important things in life existed—things like living a little longer and being well enough to enjoy her family while she is still breathing—things like being able to walk and talk and not be physically sick. And suddenly, Lauren's wish was more important than Kenzie's dream.

I watched Kenzie as we waited in line and she analyzed the situation, recognizing the gravity of Lauren's future. She knew they were both receiving a blessing and a dream come true. When we started this part of our journey, I intended for Kenzie to receive the gift of her dream and then to help make someone else's dream come true. We were swept up in the drama and excitement of Kenzie's dream, so we hadn't gotten to that part yet. But I saw a remarkable thing happen in Kenzie's heart as we stood in line at that Pennsylvania fair.

"Mom, I hope Carrie has time to give to Lauren." Kenzie was worried because it looked like the organizers were running short on time.

"Mom, we need to hurry so Lauren has more time with Carrie." Kenzie was willing to give up some of her time with Carrie for Lauren.

God had worked in my daughter's heart—to care for a stranger who had bigger needs and worries. Lauren experienced life-and-death concerns beyond my daughter's ability to comprehend their full magnitude, yet Kenzie could still empathize with another child in need. What a dream come true for this mother—my daughter felt pain and sympathy for someone else, and she wanted to make that person's life a little easier; she wanted to help make that little girl's dream come true. At that moment, I knew our journey had been a success, even if we didn't get our time with Carrie in the meet and greet event. The girl in line behind her made the difference.

Plans change. At least, our plans change. God is funny like that—He typically wants the last word. He planned a meeting between my daughter and Lauren. Lauren, who faced a life-threatening illness, became the little girl who birthed empathy in my daughter's heart. Kenzie genuinely cared about Lauren, and for the first time that day, Lauren's needs and wishes were more important than Kenzie's dream. God placed Lauren in line behind Kenzie, and my daughter was forever changed.

When Kenzie's turn with Carrie arrived, Kenzie had something on her mind besides autographs and pictures. She was thinking of the little girl in line behind her.

That night, Carrie Underwood dedicated "Jesus, Take the Wheel" to Lauren, and I saw Kenzie wipe tears from her face. Kenzie shared Carrie's desire to bless Lauren, a girl who had been through a journey of her own. My daughter's journey had intersected with that journey. None of us would ever be the same.

I heard her praying that night. She thanked God for people like Carrie Underwood and Tony Romo because they were gifts to her and made her dream come true.

About a week after we returned from the *gift of dreams* trip, Kenzie's Grammie asked her what she wanted for Christmas. Kenzie didn't hesitate to answer.

"I want Lauren to be well."

The extraordinary heroes in her life had left a mark on Kenzie—by example, they had modeled the gift of compassion for her. Thanks to their willingness to get involved in the lives of unknown children, my daughter now had a bigger heart for others.

Our journey taught us to dream big. We learned we had to be willing to believe that the impossible can happen, even in our lives. Who would've imagined that Dallas Cowboys quarterback Tony Romo would be involved in our dream come true and that American Idol Carrie Underwood would take the time to make a little girl's wish a reality? We weren't anyone "special," yet they found the time to make a difference in our lives.

Through the years, dreamers like Thomas Edison and Henry Ford have taught us that everyone has the opportunity to dream. Dream big and persevere when the first attempt falls flat. Those who have dreamed before us inspire us to reach beyond the normal limits—to try what might be difficult, even impossible.

This gift of dreams taught us that nothing is too big, nothing is too unimportant; nothing is out of the realm of possibility if our dream comes from God. We learned to trust Him and let Him author our dreams and wishes. And we learned to hope for the best, believe during times of discouragement, and experience peace when our dream is still just a dream.

We also learned to thank Him when those dreams become reality. Most of all, we learned that there are no limits with God.

Dream big, my friend, and watch what God will do.

Who would've thought that my daughter would receive more than the gift of dreams on this journey? She received so much more than a chance to meet a celebrity, a dream come true for sure—she was also given the gift of compassion.

Journey Stop
Eight

The Ultimate Gift

My dream had come true. Kenzie went on a journey unlike anything she had been on before. She touched the hearts and lives of so many. She experienced exceptional gifts that some never get the chance to experience in their entire lifetime. I count myself as one of the lucky ones, since I was given the opportunity of a lifetime as a passenger on this journey with my daughter. I was there when she discovered that there is greatness everywhere around her, and she can't buy any of it.

Kenzie grew in her journey, just as we had prayed. God had walked with us as we delivered meals to those who needed them, as we learned with other children, as we walked with the homeless on the beach, as we worked for free, as we enjoyed her friendships, as we witnessed her dream come true—only to learn that she would give that dream away in the blink of an eye if she needed to. Words can't capture the deep emotions we experienced throughout this journey.

The journey was born in my heart when Kenzie made the decision to accept Christ into her life and become a child of God. She came to her dad and me and said she wanted to meet with our pastor about being baptized. At that time, Doug and I wanted to make sure that Kenzie truly understood what a gift God is. After traveling many miles on this journey, Kenzie explained that she was ready to receive the final gift.

It was hard to imagine, but almost to the exact date, six months had passed since this journey began. Pastor Tom's face appeared on the screen as Kenzie watched what would be her last gift message.

"Kenzie, over the past weeks you've received a lot of gifts. Those gifts are wonderful; they help you to see what a wonderful world you live in and how many wonderful people are out there. You experienced many different gifts. There are all kinds of places and people from all walks of life in our world. You met many of them. The Bible talks about different gifts and explains that the greatest gift is love. The greatest gift in life is in knowing God and having a relationship with Jesus Christ based on love. All the gifts you experienced are wonderful, but one gift surpasses them—the gift that Jesus gave on the cross. He died for our sins, and God raised Him from the dead. He gives us the opportunity to believe in Him, go to Heaven with Him, and to live through all of eternity in Heaven. So when you're baptized, you wear the identification and symbol that you are a believer in Jesus Christ.

"We as the church own that sacrament together with you. We affirm you. You'll be making a lot of decisions over the course of your life, but there's one decision that is the most important one you'll ever make—asking Jesus to come into your life. It'll change the way you look at life today and the way you approach eternity. The other gifts have been a blessing, but this is the greatest gift of all. This is the *ultimate gift*."

As the television went blue, Kenzie took my hand and said, "I'm ready." Doug and I looked at Kenzie. We saw complete peace coupled with the most beautiful excitement on the face of our firstborn. We continued to encourage our daughter.

"God has blessed you. You'll face many challenges ahead, but you have many amazing people around you to help you through each one. With God in your heart, you'll never be alone. You've understood each gift so well, and this journey has made you stronger; you can now be an example for others. You have made one of our dreams come true by deciding to accept the *ultimate gift*, and you show by your actions and words that you understand there is a God and that He is awesome. So, stay true and always remember what the *ultimate gift* is in life—Jesus. He's better than anything else you'll ever receive. My challenge to you is to continue this journey and along the way, through your words and actions, I pray you'll lead others to the *ultimate gift*."

The morning arrived, and we were standing in the baptistery at our church. Our family and friends were all eagerly waiting in the sanctuary. I couldn't help but feel great pride for my daughter and gratitude for everything she learned. Before we walked to the baptistery, I prayed over Kenzie, and my heart felt as though it would beat out of my chest. As the music started, it was as if the stained glass took on a glow of its own. I stared at the screen as they played the music. All that appeared on the screen were Kenzie's bare feet waiting in the water.

I leaned against the wall, thanking God for holding me up. As she walked into the baptistery, she released my hand and never looked back, almost as if to proclaim in front of all of her family and friends, *Lord, I am yours—take me and wash me clean.* Our pastor took Kenzie's hand and led her into the water.

Kenzie's baptism was her opportunity to proclaim to others her decision to accept the *ultimate gift* of Jesus Christ. As I reflected on her willing acceptance of Jesus, I pondered our journey. Then my dream came true for her, and her true journey began as she learned to walk with Christ in this life.

This gift-giving journey has introduced her to the truth: that gifts and gift-givers surround us, and that she, too, holds a responsibility to be a gift-giver. She has the privilege of touching other lives through her journey and being a blessing to those she touches. She has witnessed greatness in the lives of otherwise ordinary people, and she has experienced greatness that comes only in knowing the God of the universe.

What an awesome God we serve—one who is willing to entrust us with His ultimate gift and allow us the privilege of traveling this journey with Him. As He has taken our hands on this journey, we've witnessed extraordinary gift-givers and simple acts of kindness that changed us. We're different. We've paused at various journey stops where He has spoken to our hearts, and we've viewed scenic outlooks along the way that have taken our breath away. God has unveiled His truths so we could glimpse a bit of His glory in the lives around us, snapshots of Heaven while we journey here. Be blessed as you gaze at our travels—as you look into our journey stops and scenic outlooks along the way—and be blessed as you come to the final destination on this journey. My hope is that you will also be changed as you discover the *ultimate gift.*

Thirty Scenic Outlooks
on the Journey
to the Ultimate Dream:
Gift-Giving Principles for the Journey

Scenic Outlook
One
Preparation for the Journey

To experience the gifts around us, we have to begin with prepared hearts—hearts that embrace the Gift-Giver and the gifts. As we embrace God, we realize His gifts are superior to anything we could imagine or hope for, and the promise of His presence and help on the journey is all we need to continue our walk in this world. Having faith in God becomes paramount to anything we can achieve or experience. The concept of "faith alone" teaches us that "God alone" is enough. He is all we need for our journey. We learn on our journey that God is who He says He is and that God will do what He promises to do. We learn to believe, and the journey becomes an experience with God. So, our preparation for the journey is simply to yield our hearts and to believe that God is enough—to have faith that God holds our hands on the journey.

Scenic Outlook
Two
Receiving the Gifts—Accepting the Challenge of the Journey

How many of us miss out on the true gifts of life because we don't see the gifts in today?

We get busy and distracted, or we focus on all the wrong things, and we miss out on the gifts right in front of us. We miss the opportunity to help a struggling neighbor or to witness the smiles on our children's faces. Take the time today to allow God to give you the eyes to see what He has in store for you—the gifts He has prepared especially for you this day.

The challenge is to be willing to go on this journey with God and others—to look at life from a different perspective. The call to open our eyes to see the gifts and to be vulnerable enough in life to experience the gifts is a journey few of us have experienced—but it's open to all. Everyone is invited to walk this journey.

Scenic Outlook
Three
Keep God First

The referee's whistle called the teams to attention. As one of our starters, I stepped onto the court, ready for the thrill that always swept over me at the opening tip-off. Basketball taught me to throw myself into life's game with passion. Playing high school basketball pushed me to dream. Wins, trophies, the roar of the crowd, and that final buzzer drove me to play the game with heart, passion, and purpose—to reach for something bigger than what I could accomplish on my own. Ultimately, basketball taught me to have faith, because a short girl faces huge obstacles when she steps onto the basketball court.

My dreams grew as my game improved, and I found myself dreaming of playing college ball—a dream that transported me into a completely different arena. When I ventured to share my dreams and my fears with my mom, she always responded with, "Follow your dreams, Heather, and remember to keep God first."

Mom taught me the importance of keeping God first, but I learned along the way that I didn't always know exactly how to put her wise words into practice. And as a mother myself, I discovered even more acutely the difficulty of the mission to keep God first. At one point as a young mother, I struggled because I felt that I needed a career. I looked for ways to meet that personal expectation and found myself unhappy and unfulfilled. Then I discovered that being Kenzie and Luke's mom was my calling. I understood my purpose to teach them about the important things in life, the simple things—contentment, faith, peace, selflessness, giving, seeing the beauty in our world, and looking for eternal treasures. As a mother, I finally grasped the meaning of "keeping God first," and I was then able to pass along that wisdom to my own children.

Scenic Outlook
Four
Seek the Ultimate Gift-Giver

When my children, Kenzie and Luke, were born, I was amazed by the way each new baby wrapped all five fingers around only one of mine. As I gazed at their tiny fingers, I pondered how they depended upon me for everything—food, safety, comfort, daily care, protection, love—all the essential needs for life. My children survived because I was there for them. I realized the significance of those quiet moments, and I understood that as they grasped my fingers, I had somebody holding my other hand. God was my source of provision as I sought to provide for my children. He was my gift-giver.

I learned to seek Him in the most difficult circumstances as well as the everyday experiences, and I desperately wanted to pass on to my children that dependence upon God. With the births of both of my children, I realized my need for His help in raising these precious gifts that He had entrusted to me. I also grew to understand my need to seek Him along the way—when my children wanted the hottest new toy at the store, as well as when Luke's doctor tested him for cystic fibrosis. The negative results brought relief, but the search for God in the middle of my pain brought a deeper understanding of the ultimate Gift-Giver. Each step of my journey has yielded a stronger dependence on God. Just as my newborns held tightly to my finger, I clung to the hand of God, and in the process, I grew to know the Gift-Giver.

We can find comfort that as our children grow and become independent, they will learn to let go of our hands and reach for the hand of God. When they release our grip and we're nowhere around, they will know to cling to the hand of the ultimate Gift-Giver.

Scenic Outlook
Five
Recognize the Source of Lasting Gifts

When I was a kid, the big event in our small Oklahoma town was coed softball. Our family spent most of our free time in the evenings playing softball with a few other families from our church community, and one family became especially close to ours. Laura was like a sister to me, and her mother, Sharon, was my mom's best friend. I was about five years old when Sharon was diagnosed with Hodgkin's disease. As we gathered each week to play ball, we watched Sharon fade with her disease. I remember being frightened—scared that my mom was losing her best friend and scared that my best friend was losing her mom. It's my earliest memory of death, and my first experience of relying on God. I also remember the peace that washed over me when I learned Sharon would be in Heaven with Jesus. He gave me the gift of Sharon and Laura, but He also introduced me to the gift of peace through Jesus. As I experienced the gifts of His help and His presence, He was planting in me the gift-giving seeds.

I didn't recognize at the time what He had in store for my future; I certainly didn't know enough to recognize and appreciate the gifts that He showered into each of my days. But the seed was planted to recognize that lasting gifts ultimately come from God.

Scenic Outlook
Six
Will It Really Matter in Sixty Years?

Third-grade worries are different from the cares we face as adults. My biggest concern as a third-grader was making the track relay team. As I fretted over the possibility of not making the team, my Papa Taylor offered me sage words of advice—"Sixty years from now, you'll never know the difference." I'm not sure I fully appreciated his wisdom at the age of eight, because I desperately wanted to be on the team, but his words still ring true in my ears today. I find myself asking that question over and over as I face grown-up worries and concerns. Will it really matter in sixty years?

We may passionately crave something today that we never receive. We may also be the recipients of things today that we don't remember past bedtime.

But the question is still the same—does it really matter? And will it matter sixty years from now?

God often surprises me by unveiling His plans one tiny step at a time, and as time passes, I stand back and see the big picture. It wasn't at all what I had planned or asked for, but the end results are so much better. Relay races are sometimes won in the first heat, but usually not. The anchor typically makes up for lost ground and turns up the speed to the "wow" level. When we learn to trust God with the details of daily living, we can more easily yield the grasp on the baton. We can learn to ask the question, "Will it really matter?" And like a third-grader handing off that baton to the next sprinter, we have the privilege of watching God carry our team across the finish line in ways we never expected.

Scenic Outlook
Seven
God Reveals His Plans Through "Yes" and "No"

Yeses are welcome in my world. It's the noes that cause alarm. My struggle is in trusting God when He says no to something I desperately want or need. Part of that struggle originates from forgetting who He is—the ultimate Gift-Giver. He is always good, always faithful, and never late. His timing is perfect. So, if He says no, He may be saying wait. God invites us to pray because sometimes the no is negotiable. Sometimes. The point is—He cares, even when He says no. God carefully orchestrates the details of our lives. Each step is planned, and every detail is important.

While it's true that we often face some difficult noes to our pleadings, we later usually discover relief or delight that He said no to our original requests. He rescues us from messes before we can get mixed up in them. He keeps us out of danger or prevents us from making foolish mistakes. He protects us from regrets. Some of the closed doors we will never understand, but we can be confident that the God of the universe knows what He's doing, and maybe someday He'll let us in on the mystery. Until then, we can trust Him in the noes and rejoice in the yeses. Each yes and each no is a gift. We just have to open our spiritual eyes to see them.

Scenic Outlook
Eight
God Opens Our Eyes to See the Gifts

Kids don't usually recognize the gifts around them. Neither do adults. We tend to get lost in our worlds, pursuing the latest and greatest this world has to offer. We think gifts have a price tag and can be purchased by a credit card; we assume the sparkle of a new material object will provide satisfaction and happiness. We're deceived into believing that the next new thing will finally make us feel complete. But we're blind to the gifts around us, the true gifts that will impact us for eternity. True, lasting gifts are everywhere, and we often don't recognize the gifts until God opens our eyes to see them.

While my dream to play college basketball drove me to reach for what some would call an impossible goal for a short girl, I stretched beyond what my fears defined as boundaries and what others considered possible. I made it. I made the college team. My heart still raced at the referee's whistle and the starting buzzer. But by college, I had begun to see and receive the lasting, intangible gifts God offers. And I discovered I was content to sit on the bench because I was different. The gift was in being a part of the team. God was first, and the team mattered more than my individual accomplishments. God gave me the gift to see what really mattered and to accept the gift He had for me.

Scenic Outlook
Nine
Adopting a "Grandparents" Attitude

"Joe, do you want any dessert?" Nannie asked Papa Taylor the same question each Sunday when my family had lunch with them.

"One of each." Papa's reply was always the same.

Nannie pretended to be bothered by his greediness, but with a smile on her face, she served him "one of each."

Similar moments with my other grandparents often trigger a smile. As we'd leave Grandma Bea and Grandpa Moore's house, we'd hear them say, "Y'all come back," as they hugged us at the back door. The words are still a reminder of the special times we spent on the back porch swinging and having heartfelt talks with them. Times have changed and life is different, but the memories of time spent with grandparents are priceless.

I'm daily challenged to approach life with Papa Taylor's attitude—"give me one of each"—to the gifts God has prepared for me. I remind myself that the "y'all come back" greetings won't last forever. Developing the attitude that time is priceless enriches our lives. My grandparents taught me to love and receive love, a reflection of the love we share in Christ. And if we could grasp the magnitude of His goodness and the riches of His true gifts, we'd be blessed beyond our imagination. If we had the eyes to see and the hearts to receive, we could experience the greatness of His bounty as we walk through this life.

Scenic Outlook
Ten
Everyone Is Touched on the Journey

As Kenzie experienced each journey stop, I was thrilled with the growth I witnessed in her life. She became more sensitive to others, while also becoming more aware of the gifts and opportunities around her. This was my goal. The added benefit was that Kenzie wasn't the only person affected by our journey—many others were touched along the way.

I learned to grow in faith, patience, and perseverance. I saw that sharing our story impacted those who listened. Joy and peace became a part of my daily life on the journey. When each day began, I felt excitement about what God would do that day. I learned to anticipate the wonders of a very big God.

Luke was also touched by our journey. He witnessed Kenzie's journey stops and expressed excitement for her. He joined in our conversations along the way, sharing what he had learned through each experience. Not only was Luke blessed by the journey, but my friends, family, and even strangers were blessed as well.

Scenic Outlook
Eleven
Give Your Children Opportunities to Use Their Gifts

As parents, we're sometimes tempted to step in and intervene when our kids are involved in new activities. We want to cushion their experience and control the outcome—but wait. Sit back and watch. Let your children figure out how to make things happen, and you'll find in the course of that discovery that they'll learn how to make a difference in others' lives. The process causes them to grow and discover their own giftedness. They develop confidence and the assurance that they are equipped for the work they've been given.

Kenzie learned this as she tried to read with Hope. She later confided to me that she just kept trying to find a way to reach her. Hope finally came and sat next to her, and Kenzie said, "At that moment, I knew I had done it." Kenzie grew in confidence when she realized she could do something that even I as an adult wasn't able to accomplish. She also recognized that many more opportunities exist to make a difference in someone's life—maybe even another Hope.

Our children want to be successful; they want to experience the satisfaction of accomplishing something meaningful, even if it's difficult. That's where our role as parents changes from guide to encourager to observer. We learn to sit back and watch our children

75

as they figure out how to do something difficult, how they can stretch beyond their limits, how to discover and use their talents and gifts, and how to touch the Hopes of the world. All these challenges make a difference.

Scenic Outlook
Twelve
Destination: Greatness

"Greatness" isn't what we think. It isn't a place of honor or prestige. It isn't being important or well known. It isn't having a showcase of trophies and awards to put on display. It isn't acting self-righteous or snobbish. Greatness is becoming everything God intended us to be—and we become that when we give our lives to Jesus.

We prepare our kids for college, we train them in athletic disciplines, and we groom them for success— all for the pursuit of greatness. Yet, Kenzie and I learned along our journey stops that greatness isn't something we achieve. "Great" is what we become as we yield our lives to God and give ourselves to others. As our character changes to reflect the character of gift-givers, we experience true greatness.

Scenic Outlook
Thirteen
Encourage Gratitude

The movie theater was packed with kids. Kenzie's friends enjoyed her birthday party almost as much as Kenzie did. As Kenzie unwrapped presents, she thanked friends for each card and gift. As the kids settled in to enjoy the movie, Kenzie found me.

"Mom, thanks for doing this—I know it was a lot of work."

Seeing Kenzie take the time to stop giggling and chatting with friends to demonstrate gratefulness to her parent was an encouragement. If she could remind herself to be grateful in the middle of a party and then follow through with the act of thanking someone, I knew she was learning from our journey.

Even adults have a difficult time expressing gratitude when they are somewhat preoccupied with friends, gifts, and activities. They may have good intentions to write a note or make a phone call later, but time gets away so often, and the thank-you is often never expressed. I was encouraged by Kenzie's act of maturity in deliberately going out of her way to thank someone.

As parents, we too often ignore those available moments to teach our children to express gratitude; we get busy with the urgency of the present activity and hope that our children will one day grow up enough to have manners and demonstrate thoughtfulness.

Most of the time it takes a little prompting from us to encourage our children to take the initiative to reach out to others and put their gratitude into words. Teaching our children to say thank you is a gift.

Scenic Outlook
Fourteen
Give Thanks for the People
Behind the Scenes

Many people who never met my daughter became gift-givers in her life. And still others who knew Kenzie were willing to work quietly behind the scenes to bless her.

Others were also behind the scenes on many gifts. Kenzie's principal helped set the stage for delivering the message to Kenzie. My husband Doug worked to arrange the flight and hotel as soon as we got the news that the *gift of dreams* was going to be a reality. He enjoyed getting every detail in place for this trip—not a position of much thanks when everyone is scurrying around with excitement and anticipation, but his contribution to our comfort and our journey was essential to making the dream come true.

We arrived in Pennsylvania. As Kenzie and I stood by the orange privacy fence surrounding the area between the concert arena and Carrie Underwood's tour bus, Kenzie and I discussed Carrie's behind-the-scenes helpers. Hair and makeup people, bus drivers, band members, event organizers, and promoters all help Carrie arrive at her tour stops, prepared and ready to touch lives. Everyone needs help, and we all have those individuals who use their gifts and talents in the background, contributing to our lives and cheering us on along our way.

Not only do we have behind-the-scenes helpers, we too, can become willing participants as blessing-providers to others. We can learn to be behind-the-scenes helpers as prayer warriors for others—doing battle in prayer on their behalf for the heartaches and struggles that our loved ones face. Behind-the-scenes heroes have eyes to see practical needs in others' lives—cooking a meal for an ill friend, driving a neighbor's child to school, and mowing the yard of an elderly family member. Doing the often unnoticed task is typical for a service-minded friend. Sometimes the behind-the-scenes heroes are just good listeners; they hold your hand when you cry, and they listen with sensitivity to your pain. They don't offer tired clichés to bandage your wounds. No one may ever see or know what sacrifice was made, but we can all look quietly for ways to make a difference.

Behind-the-scenes heroes aren't in the limelight. They don't look for applause; in fact, the accolades probably make them a bit uncomfortable. But the knowledge that they have blessed others is enough. And the recipient's awareness of their hero's sacrifices and the offering of a warm thank-you are usually welcome.

Scenic Outlook
Fifteen
Heroes, Extraordinary and Ordinary

Rain poured as I hurried into the school to find Kenzie. With her shirt still tucked in and her hair bow bouncing on her head, she handed me a piece of paper. Shielding the paper from the rain, we ran to the car, avoiding puddles along the way. She explained the note as we waited in the line of cars to leave the school.

"The PTA Reflection Program leaders want us to paint pictures. The theme is 'A Different Kind of Hero.'" Kenzie beamed as she talked about the project.

Later that week, while Luke and his dad roughhoused in the living room, Kenzie sat at the kitchen table working on her painting. I tried to catch a glimpse of her artwork, but I made myself stay away so she could create without distraction.

"Mom, I'm done." Kenzie smiled and sat back as she looked over her painting one more time.

"Beautiful, Kenzie! Who is it?"

"Mom, it's you!" Kenzie had painted me in a shirt with a big red heart on it, with arms outstretched. The caption read, "My Mom, My Hero."

I was humbled, proud, and flattered that my daughter would call me her hero. I also felt a call to live up to that name.

Hero. We attach so many meanings to that word— superman, conqueror, inspiration, example, savior, leader, champion, model, idol, star, and deliverer. How can we ever live up to that description? We can't. We have to let the true Savior and Deliverer—Jesus Christ—work in us to conform us to His image. True heroes know their limitations, and they know where to go for strength.

I would say I'm a pretty ordinary hero. There is nothing unusual about me. Not many people recognize me when I go to Wal-Mart, and paparazzi don't follow me flashing their cameras with my every move. But ordinary heroes know how to make a difference daily in others' lives.

As Kenzie grew out of her my-mommy-is-my-hero stage, she became enthralled with Carrie Underwood— an extraordinary hero. I assure you she can't walk into Wal-Mart unnoticed. Carrie uses her fame to inspire others, and she's not shy about giving glory to God. Her willingness to meet the children, to give hugs, and to wait patiently while pictures were snapped was a gift to the kids at the meet and greet that day. The impact of this extraordinary hero on my daughter has been lasting.

What would it take for all of us to become heroes? Tony Romo, Carrie Underwood, and my mother all have this in common—they're heroes. And we can learn from them; we can attempt to become heroes in our worlds. Becoming a hero requires only a few things: using our gifts and talents wholeheartedly, living lives of integrity, and genuinely caring for others. No glitter or drum rolls are required. No front-page press releases. Just concern for others and living a life worth mimicry.

One of my earliest memories is seeing my mother reading her Bible. That image is imprinted in my mind, and it continues to challenge me to live out my faith in front of my children—to be a role model to them, as my mother was to me.

When I left for college, Mom gave me a letter with those words that still inspire me to be more than I can ever be—you're my hero. Not long ago, my daughter said those same words to me: you're my hero. And even while I struggle to live up to the meaning of those words, I'm inspired to use my gifts to bless others, to be an example to those who watch, and to care for others. I'm urged to act like a hero. I'm compelled to become a hero.

Scenic Outlook
Sixteen
Be Available When
the Brokenhearted Come

On the California beach in his ministry to the homeless, Pastor Rick was an example of selfless giving, and Kenzie and I both learned from him. Watching him made us stop and wonder if we could look for ways to be more useful in service to others. So we asked ourselves some hard questions.

When someone has a need, even though it may not be the most convenient time for me, am I available?

It may be the only time someone reaches out. I may be their last hope, their last attempt at asking for help. Am I willing to give my time and energy? Am I willing to be inconvenienced? Am I willing to set aside my own schedule and give someone else priority in this moment of need? Do I welcome interruptions, even though the timing may not be what I would've planned or chosen? When the need arises, am I eager to step in and make a difference?

Two weeks before Christmas, the kids and I were decorating the house and baking cookies—a Christmas tradition. The temperature was freezing, and we shared that cozy, warm feeling that comes with hot chocolate commercials. Christmas was in the air.

"Mom, who buys gifts for the kids at school who can't afford gifts?"

"Well, some of them don't receive gifts, but the more fortunate kids become an angel for the Angel Tree. You know, this weekend we picked out angels to shop for."

The kids raced to our tree to look at their angel ornaments.

"I want to know everything it says about my angel," Kenzie said.

"Me too," Luke chimed in.

Kenzie and Luke grabbed crayons to make cards for their angels. The next day we went shopping and picked out everything their angels requested. Kenzie and Luke learned that giving to their angels was one way to be there for the brokenhearted, a new favorite Christmas tradition.

We all have opportunities to make a difference in others' lives. My kids have enjoyed packing shoeboxes full of goodies at Christmas for kids who don't have even the basic necessities like toothbrushes and socks. Serving Thanksgiving meals, delivering food to the homebound elderly, giving rides to the disabled—we have plenty of opportunities to learn the blessing of being inconvenienced. We can offer a listening ear to those who grieve. We can learn to be quiet and comfort those in distress by simply being present, bearing their burdens by being there. And we can learn from Pastor Rick how to be available when the brokenhearted come.

Scenic Outlook
Seventeen
A Bible and a Bike

When Kenzie and I met William on the beach, we learned a lesson about reaching out to the needy—in this case, a homeless needy person. When William challenged us with his question: "What do you think I need most out here?" and Kenzie and I both assumed the answer to be a Bible—remember his startling answer? "No, a bike." His bike helped him survive.

It was a reminder to us that even though we want to tell others about Jesus and we want to lead them to God, sometimes the best avenue isn't by bringing out the Bible. Sometimes people learn more about Jesus when we give them a bike—something they really, desperately need to survive. As we seek to share the gospel message with others, we can learn from Mother Teresa's method—meeting practical needs as an expression of Christ's love.

Necessities in life don't always fit into a nice, neat, molded box. Christians would declare the urgent necessity of sharing Bible verses, but sometimes others can't hear the wisdom of those verses until we first give them a bike. The bike may be the only tool that invites another to listen to the Bible. If we aren't willing to meet practical needs like food, shelter, job, and transportation, then our needy friends might close their hearts to the message of the Bible. So the next time you feel compelled to share the gospel with someone, find out if they need a bike first.

Scenic Outlook
Eighteen
Give God the Glory

"We will give God the glory when we lose, and we will give God the glory when we win." Coach Grant Hayes in the movie, *Facing the Giants*, challenged his team with that statement. Like a well-worn football, I tucked that thought away and have retrieved it many times throughout our journey.

We were seven weeks into Kenzie's ultimate journey. She still had some gifts to experience, and I was still trying to make a few of them happen.

One morning as I said goodbye to the kids at school, I dropped my cell phone between my seats. When I pulled into my driveway, I dug around to retrieve my phone. In the process, I also pulled out a crumpled piece of paper—my original plans for Kenzie's journey.

I sat with my car door open, looking over long-forgotten details of my budding plan. It resembled a coach's play sheet. The front and back were covered in ideas, numbers, contacts, dates, and times. I thought about how some of the plans were right on time, some completely changed, and some never happened.

I climbed my porch stairs and sat on the rocking chair. I remembered how some of the details worked out from beginning to end. I felt sad that a few of my plans never came to pass, or at least I didn't think they did at the time. But I realized that no matter how difficult this journey had been, I always gave God the glory. As the coach admonishes his team in the movie, I had to remind myself—no matter what happens, give God the glory, whether in loss or triumph.

The biggest challenge was with the *gift of dreams*. It hadn't happened yet, and I didn't think it was going to come to fruition. I was exhausted trying to arrange the opportunity for Kenzie to give her hero—Carrie Underwood—a hug. I guessed this one just wasn't in the cards. I had tried; I had prayed continually. I finally came to the point where I relinquished my hold on that gift, realizing that no matter what happened with that gift, it was out of my control. I'd done everything I could. God was the only One who could make it happen. It was too big for me. I thanked Him for all the blessings and guidance He had provided during the last seven weeks of Kenzie's journey. I stepped into the house and started cleaning.

God later surprised us. Kenzie received her gift of dreams from the ultimate Gift-Giver. We were blessed, and only God could've pulled it off.

Just as Carrie Underwood was willing to publicly acknowledge God along her journey, we too can give God the glory as we journey. Giving glory to God doesn't mean we're singing a constant hallelujah chorus—it simply means we acknowledge and proclaim Him as the One who deserves the praise and applause for everything in life. Our travels may not put us in the public spotlight, but we have the opportunity to touch our little corner of the world by giving God glory when we interact with the one or two people who come into our lives today. We can offer our appreciation to our faithful God, whether we win or lose.

Scenic Outlook
Nineteen
Who's in Line with You?

We stood in line to get into the American Idol concert. As we waited to see Carrie Underwood,

Kenzie and I made small talk with a couple in line with us—two ordinary, friendly people. Then we discovered they were Carrie Underwood's parents. Why were they standing in line like the rest of the crowd? Didn't they get special privileges? I was amazed that they approached their daughter's fame with such down-to-earth humility. They even obliged Kenzie and posed for a picture with her.

I'm reminded of the times in the Bible when ordinary people's lives were touched by angels unaware—angels who appeared in the flesh, who intervened in miraculous ways, who carried on small talk. I wonder how many times we interact with others without realizing who they are, what kind of positions they hold, what kind of influence they possess, and how they impact a larger sphere.

Would it make a difference in how we treated them or how we interacted with them? I wonder how it would change the way we treat others if we thought they could be someone special. I wonder if we treated everyone as if they were someone special, what kind of impact it would have on them.

So next time you're in the grocery store line or you're waiting to get into a concert, be kind. The person in line with you may just be an angel.

Or at least some famous person's parents.

Scenic Outlook
Twenty
Eternal Gifts vs. Temporal Gifts

The den at my parents' house smelled like coffee and cinnamon rolls when my kids bounced into the room that Easter morning. I enjoyed making Easter an elaborate event for Luke and Kenzie, complete with clues in eggs left by the Easter Bunny. The Easter baskets I prepared for my kids were sensational. They were packed with Game Boys, games and designer shirts—treasures resembling gifts at a lavish event rather than reminders of a sacred holiday. High-dollar stuff. No simple chocolate bunny. No dyed Easter eggs. No Easter storybook. And Kenzie brought me to my senses.

"Jesus has risen! He's the real reason for Easter—He's alive, He's alive today!" Kenzie danced around the room with her proclamation, leaving the material gifts strewn by the basket where she had opened and quickly forgotten them. She knew what was really important that day, and she taught me a lesson: it doesn't matter what's in the basket. In my efforts to bless my children, I had focused on giving temporal gifts rather than emphasizing the lasting treasures of our celebration.

We started new traditions—sunrise service on Easter morning, celebrating our risen Lord, and telling the story of Jesus. We also shifted our focus at Christmas. Last Christmas, we gathered with my parents in the mountains, and we baked a birthday cake for Jesus and sang "Happy Birthday" to Him. The kids love it. And I love what they are learning— that some eternal treasures are more valuable than material possessions. The wrapped gifts mean so little in comparison to the blessings God has for us.

Even in day-to-day living, I've adjusted my mind-set—buying gifts for the kids has always been fun, but I've looked for other ways to enrich their lives: story time at the library, play days at the park, maybe even just time with friends and family. Those are the real treasures—the lasting gifts I can give my children, gifts of service and self rather than gifts that will fade and break. These are experiences that impact them for a lifetime. I've learned to value the things God values, and I'm teaching my children to make choices that last for eternity.

Scenic Outlook
Twenty-One
What Gift-Givers Surround You?

Seven o'clock and the kids are just waking. Kenzie hasn't felt well in a few days, but Doug and I are determined to get everyone dressed and out the door for church by 9:15. The smell of blueberry muffins fills the house—the family is visiting.

Kenzie's excited that she is moving up a grade level in Sunday school; Luke shares the anticipation of a new, more mature class. We file into the church building at 9:10, and the kids run to their new classes and greet old friends. The youth minister waves a hello to Kenzie from across the hall. Doug and I hurry to our class.

After church, we eat lunch together and head home to clean out closets. Kenzie and Luke decide to make room in their closets by weeding out old toys. Kenzie discovers she has too many stuffed animals and decides to give more bears to the bear ministry she learned about in the *gift of giving.*

Luke leaves with his dad to play baseball with some T-ball teammates, while Kenzie curls up with a book. I start dinner. After dinner, the kids help clear the table, and we all head toward bed. As I tuck Kenzie into bed, she says she feels much better after resting today.

I put my feet up while sipping a cup of coffee and think about our day. In that one day, my kids experienced a number of gifts. Gift-givers surrounded them. Kenzie and Luke enjoyed the gift of family through extended family and our own immediate family. They experienced the gift of work at church through the gifts of Sunday school workers and pastors, by helping each other clean out closets, and by helping clear the table after dinner. The kids participated in the gift of giving when they chose to give away toys. The lessons taught that morning at church, as well as Kenzie's reading and Luke's learning at baseball practice, were a part of the gift of learning. Church and T-ball practice provided the gift of friends. Kenzie experienced the gift of healing when she began to feel better that afternoon, after a few days of illness. The kids are daily surrounded by the gift of love from family, friends, church, Doug, and me.

Wow, seven gifts in one day. When we stop and take inventory, I think we can all see how we are surrounded by gifts and gift-givers as we journey through life. Who can we learn from? What unique gifts do the people around us have? What gifts surround us? We need moments such as these to slow down and ponder and see with new eyes the blessings of gift-giving in our lives—lives packed with Game Boys and designer shirts, treasures resembling gifts at a lavish event rather than reminders of a sacred holiday. High-dollar stuff. No simple chocolate bunny. No dyed Easter eggs. No Easter storybook. And Kenzie brought me to my senses.

Scenic Outlook
Twenty-Two
The Beginning and the End

Luke was sick on and off almost from the day he was born. This day was no different. He labored to breathe, but I wasn't worried too much.

After the doctor examined Luke, however, fear gripped my heart.

"We need to run more tests. Luke is presenting symptoms of cystic fibrosis."

We discussed what that meant, and I asked the question that haunted me: "What is the life expectancy for people with cystic fibrosis?"

"Maybe twenty."

Chaos filled the room as nurses came back with scheduled test dates and times. Kenzie couldn't understand why I was crying. Everything had changed for me when I had walked into the doctor's office. I now faced the possibility of losing my child.

In my panic, I was determined to take Luke anywhere to get the help he needed, to find a cure, to experience healing. Doug and I called our family, friends, and church to ask for prayer.

The test was negative—no cystic fibrosis. But the experience of facing the possibility of tragedy compelled me to look at life differently.

I've witnessed birth and death. I've watched loved ones take their first breath, and I've cried as others have taken their last. Life is about beginnings and endings. We have precious little time to make our lives count, to touch others, to bless others, to make a difference in our world. Each day is a new beginning with the certainty of an ending. What matters is what we do with the time in between.

Scenic Outlook
Twenty-Three
Nurture

I hurried to the hospital because Nannie—my grandmother—was dying. I walked into the room to see my father holding his mother's hand and whispering gently to her. He sold his business and spent the past two years taking care of her as her health declined, and now he nurtured his mother as she died.

We often think of nurturing as something a mother does with her children. The word "nurturing" conjures up the image of a soft-spoken mother stroking her young child's hair at bedtime or spooning soup into a sick child's mouth. But learning to nurture others is something we can all learn, as my father so vividly demonstrated to me.

We nurture others by caring enough to listen when they're lonely or hurt. We nurture faith by encouraging the downhearted. We nurture as we offer a gift of service to someone who needs a hand. Offering a nurturing heart to others is an enduring gift.

Scenic Outlook
Twenty-Four
My Best Friend, Mom

Mom and I were driving to Oklahoma City in search of a wedding dress—mine. During my almost one-year engagement, Mom and I spent a lot of time together. On this particular drive, we talked about our expectations for my wedding plans—date, time, flowers, attendants, place—the usual wedding stuff. Who did I want to perform the ceremony? I thrilled my mom when I asked her what she thought about me using the same preacher who performed her wedding ceremony. As her only daughter, I offered her that gift.

Mom was there for me as I grew up—games, performances, parties, and life. She shared in my experiences, making them richer by her presence. She sent me encouraging letters in college, and she visits my family often today. If we can't see each other, we talk by phone. Mom is my best friend.

I was reminded of this as I sat in church one Sunday morning. A crinkled and stained letter dated December 1997 fell out of my Bible. I heard Mom's voice as I read the familiar encouraging words: "I'm proud of you and your brother. Always pursue your dreams. Dad and I will always love you unconditionally. Remember to keep God first." Reminders of her steadfast love, and affirmations of who I was, will always be precious words from my best friend, Mom.

Scenic Outlook
Twenty-Five
The Importance of Dad

Men crowded the halls outside Kenzie's kindergarten class on Dad's Day. Kids everywhere beamed, overjoyed that they could show off their favorite man—Dad. Kenzie was no exception.

The kids had spent a lot of time preparing for this special day by putting out rugs, setting up Sprite stations and games, and displaying artwork and paintings. They eagerly anticipated the moment their dads would arrive.

Men in suits, khaki slacks, gym clothes, and jeans filed in and found their children. Fill-in "dads" and grandfathers also made their entrances. One little girl, Avery, didn't have a dad, and no one came for her.

"My dad can be her dad." Kenzie quickly offered to share her father on this special day.

And my husband Doug willingly adopted Avery for the day. Avery needed someone to fill that position for her, and my husband's nature is to jump in and do what's needed. He has a heart to touch kids' lives.

Doug doesn't wait for Dad's Day to become involved in our children's lives, either. He doesn't hesitate to volunteer at church, to coach a basketball or football team, to participate in parents' conferences with teachers, or to take the kids for their shots. (I can't handle watching my kids squirm in pain.) He's an involved dad because he knows the impact he has on our children. He knows he can make a difference for a lifetime by being there today.

Dads make a difference by actively living their faith—by being that role model kids can look up to. A wise dad is an initiator in activities, but he also knows when it's best to be a behind-the-scenes influence. He prays. He believes God, and he makes decisions based on his faith. He knows how to teach his kids that God is real, God is good, and God cares about every detail of their lives.

My dad is a thinker. His willingness to take his time to answer reflects careful consideration and deep thought. I sometimes wish I were more like him— able to control my tongue and think before I speak. Watching his thoughtful responses has taught me to be careful with how I answer others, to let silence do its work before I offer my thoughts. Dad also taught me the importance of honoring my parents—not by lecturing me on the benefits of obedience, but by example. I witnessed his consistent care for his own mother while she was dying. He was there for her, and he taught me more through his actions than he ever could in a well-honed lecture. He demonstrated by example what was really important in life.

Our culture sometimes makes dads the butt of jokes—the klutz who needs rescuing by a sarcastic female or wise-mouthed kid. And while women and children have their own unique gifts to enrich our families, so do dads. We can't overlook the importance of a dad's influence in the home.

Dads often know how to challenge their kids to reach or stretch beyond their horizons. The maleness, the Y chromosome, the testosterone, the different approach to life—whatever it is, dad's uniqueness is sometimes the special factor in establishing a well-rounded home. Dads can laugh at mud puddles more easily than moms—that laid-back sense of humor completes the family and provides a humanness that mom alone may struggle to present. Dad's bark may inspire kids to action quicker than mom's threats. Mom is vital in her children's lives, but a dad's influence helps kids become everything God designed them to be.

Scenic Outlook
Twenty-Six
Be That Safe Place and Give Freedom

As a child, I could roam and play with few worries. I remember the feeling of running barefoot and not having to be somewhere. My parents didn't have to worry about kidnappings or abductions, much less teaching their children about stranger danger. Life was simple. Life was safe.

Our kids may not be able to roam freely around their neighborhoods these days, but we can provide a safe place for them. As parents, we are their safe place.

Can our kids exhale around us? Do we give them the freedom to try new things, even if they may fail? Do they feel safe enough to tell us about their mistakes, fears, and shortcomings?

Do our kids experience relief in our presence, or do they dread our reactions?

Doug and I spent our tenth anniversary on the white, pristine beaches in Cozumel. It was paradise until a hurricane hit on the third day. The island flooded; we had no phones and no electricity. Bottled water was our only option. Food was spoiling. We tried to flee our resort. Water gushed through the glove compartment and poured on my legs as the taxi attempted to drive through high water. We arrived at the airport only to discover that it was underwater.

We found a phone and got through to my brother in Oklahoma; he had been looking at our options. Fifteen minutes was our window of time to get to the ferry that would transport us to Cancun before another wave of storms hit the island. With all the drama of prime-time news specials, we made it.

I remember the impact of seeing a dry runway and feeling safe again—relief. I could finally relax. That's how our kids should feel with us—safe.

And while we want our children to feel safe with us, we also want to give them freedom to stretch and grow. I remember an incident when Kenzie wanted to go to a sleepover with an unfamiliar friend; the uncomfortable feelings of fear that washed over me made me want to clutch tightly to my precious daughter. The incident unfolded like most children's requests, with a lot of begging.

"Please, Mom, can I spend the night with Lizzie?" Kenzie whined. School had started two weeks earlier, and Kenzie had just met the girl. I wasn't comfortable with the situation. So instead, I invited neighborhood kids to our home to give her the opportunity to get to know them. I was being overprotective. Ultimately, I wasn't giving God the control in my parenting.

I could've handled the situation better. I had options: Kenzie could take more time to get to know Lizzie, or I could've invited the family over to get to know them. Instead, I had chosen to be the neighborhood watchdog.

At some point, I realized Kenzie needed some independence from me. She needed freedom to learn to make decisions, to try new experiences, and to grow. These are essential for kids as they mature. Kenzie needed the freedom to make mistakes, to explore, to look at life's options, to find out who she is, and to discover her unique gifts and talents. An anonymous writer once said, "Our greatest glory is not in never falling, but in rising every time we fall."

Ultimately, the decisions she makes are out of my control. I can influence her by being an example and living my faith honestly before her, but she has to own her faith. I have to trust that the morals and values I've taught her will carry her. Giving her freedom allows her the opportunity to grow her own faith.

Someone once said, "Parenthood is the art of bringing up children without putting them down." As we relinquish our hold on their lives and give them the necessary freedom to grow and mature, we are allowing them opportunities to become all God intended them to be. It takes wisdom to know when we should be that safe place and when we should get out of the way to give them freedom to stretch and grow.

Scenic Outlook
Twenty-Seven
Overcoming Hurdles

Discouragement. Busyness. Fatigue. Stress. Distractions. Good things that replace the best things. Misplaced priorities. The appeal of temporal, material possessions. All of these are hurdles to overcome on our journey to greatness, all demand determined perseverance—the ability to forge ahead despite the obstacles.

Overcoming hurdles requires us to see the greatness in our worlds, rather than focusing on the negatives. When Kenzie realized that no matter what, she could choose to be a giver in the world, she became empowered. No one could take away her freedom to give to others.

Kenzie's principal had a motivational plaque in her office with three words displayed prominently: courage, challenge, and perseverance. To challenge, one needs to dare to confront what can only be imagined. Kenzie learned these principles in her journey as she was challenged to overcome hurdles.

Thomas Edison once said, "Our greatest weakness lies in giving up. The most certain way to succeed is always to try one more time." The essence of perseverance is trying one more time.

Problems will always exist. Hunger, poverty, drugs, crime—the bad stuff looms. But there's so much more to give. When an obstacle pops up, my children can find a way around it. The journey has taught me that, as a mother, I may not always be able to remove the obstacles from my children's lives. Problems or fears will come. That's life. But I can stand by my children and coach them—I can help them discover who to ask for help or how to jump over or knock down the obstacle. I can partner with my children as they discover their giftedness in overcoming hurdles.

Facing obstacles teaches us to keep on, to persevere. Perseverance has many faces. We often think of it as determination and endurance. But sometimes perseverance simply comes down to survival. Take one day at a time, and keep going. Just survive. Keep on. And somewhere down the road, you realize you've stayed the course—you've persevered.

Doug and I had been married about seven months. We were visiting his parents, sitting in the living room watching a basketball game, when the phone rang. It was my mom.

"Heather, Uncle Larry just called. Julie's gone." Mom's voice broke, and sobs took over the conversation. My cousin Julie had suffered a seizure and died. "Meet Dad and me at Grandma's so we can tell her and Papa."

That day changed our family. Someone we loved was gone. My mother's sister lost her daughter. My grandmother lost a granddaughter. My mother lost a niece. I lost a cousin. For days, weeks, and months, we supported Aunt Sue, Uncle Larry, and my cousins, Jamie and Chuck. And they survived. They kept on.

Aunt Sue visits Julie's grave every Memorial Day. Thirteen years. She still misses Julie, but she hasn't let sorrow rob her of life and others of the gifts she offers. She has experienced the deepest grief a parent can feel, and yet, she doesn't let the pain paralyze her. She perseveres.

Scenic Outlook
Twenty-Eight
Become a Gift-Giver

March Madness was at its peak. It was Tuesday night of the NCAA women's basketball tournament. My favorite team—the Tennessee Lady Volunteers—was playing in the regional tournament about seventy miles from my house. Kenzie and I watched as Tennessee led the game.

For years, I followed Coach Pat Summitt and the Lady Volunteers through championship after championship. While I was drawn to the traditions of the university, Coach Summitt inspired me because she displayed an incredible ability to teach the team determination, desire, hard work, and what it takes to become champions. Coach Summitt was one of my heroes.

At halftime, Kenzie looked at me and said, "Mom, isn't this game being played at Oklahoma City?"

"Well, yes, but I didn't go because we had things to do for school." It soon became apparent just how much Kenzie had grown through her journey.

"Mom, haven't you always wanted to meet Coach Summitt?" Kenzie took my hand and looked at me with sparkling eyes. "If they win tonight, let's get tickets for the next game."

"Chances of meeting the coach are nil to none, honey."

"If you don't try, you don't have a chance." Kenzie was persistent. "Mom, I will give you the gift of dreams. Let's go to Oklahoma City, and just maybe you'll get a chance to say hello."

After the game and Tennessee's win, I kissed the kids goodnight and talked to Doug about my conversation with Kenzie. I was touched by her desire to be a gift-giver to me.

Amid the next morning's rush to get lunches together and take the kids to school, Kenzie asked me about the game again. When she climbed out of the car, she looked at me and said, "Mom, let's do it."

Throughout the day, I thought about Kenzie's desire to bless me with this gift. Just going to the game would be a gift, whether I met the coach or not, and

Kenzie would get a blessing for being a gift-giver. Then I had an idea—what if I took some copies of *The Ultimate Gift* to give to the Tennessee team? I went by Jim Stovall's office, and he gave me some copies of the book; he even signed Coach Summitt's copy.

Kenzie and I headed off to Oklahoma City for my gift of dreams. I explained to Kenzie along the way that I would have to find the correct person to deliver the books to—NCAA regulations limited gifts to players. I prayed God would lead me to just the right person.

People dressed in orange swarmed the Ford Center in Oklahoma City. After picking up our tickets at will call, I noticed three ladies, orange from head to toe. I introduced myself to them and told them about our journey and our desire to distribute books to the team. They were quick to help.

"We're having a pep rally down the street at four o'clock this afternoon. The athletic director will be there—she'll know the right person to give the books to." God had placed them directly in our path.

Orange balloons cascaded from the ceiling and hung on doors and chairs everywhere. Fans donned orange shirts, shorts, and hats. *Why didn't I wear orange?* I bought orange basketball beads in my attempt to blend in.

The band belted out "Rocky Top," and the rally was underway. The athletic director was first on the agenda. As she headed out the door, I caught up with her and explained my situation. She told me to meet her and another person by the bus in a few minutes. So Kenzie and I delivered the books to them; the athletic director shared words of encouragement with Kenzie and thanked us for our thoughtful gesture. I had to leave the rest of my dream, to meet the coach and the team, with the books. I couldn't make the dream happen—I had done all I could.

After the Tennessee win, Kenzie said, "Hurry, Mom. If we make it over to our side, they might come and sign autographs. Hurry, Mom."

We hurried over to the Tennessee side and stood on the front row as the players cut down the net. I didn't see them do it, though, because I was so in awe of my daughter's desire to give me the gift of dreams. As Coach Summitt walked off the floor, Kenzie's face fell.

"I'm sorry, Mom, that you didn't get your dream tonight."

I hugged Kenzie and smiled. "Yes, I did, honey. You have become quite a gift-giver, and that's the best dream of all."

Scenic Outlook
Twenty-Nine
Create a Gift-Giving Journey for Your Child

Planning the ultimate vacation opened my eyes to the complexities of event planning. My first vacation-planning experience centered on Disney World in

Orlando, Florida. I bought a travel book and spent hours on the internet researching the options, prices, eateries, hotels, flights, parades, parking, and events. I soon realized I was in over my head. I called a friend who had already experienced the ultimate vacation and asked for her opinions and recommendations. Three weeks later, we climbed on a plane and flew to Florida, ready to experience Disney's best. It was a magical vacation.

Two years later, I encountered a similar magical experience with Kenzie—the ultimate journey. Seven gifts, seven ways to show my child she is capable of giving and receiving gifts in her life everyday, and the blessings are magical.

I've listed the seven steps to creating a gift-giving journey for your child. Be encouraged, it takes less time than planning a vacation.

- Decide which gifts you want to give your child.
- Establish contact with gift-givers, gather props and supplies, and make the videos.
- Choose a gift a day or a gift a week.
- Arrange your schedule to accommodate your child's journey experiences.
- Make it happen.
- Be with your child to receive and experience each gift.
- Know that God is the ultimate gift.

I wanted to give Kenzie something that only time and love could buy; I wanted our journey to be an inspiration to her. Kenzie grew through the journey, and

107

her world was impacted as a result. Our kids now think and talk differently. They have eyes to see that they are surrounded every day by gifts and gift-givers; the gifts in their lives are just in a different form than usual. No longer wrapped in shiny paper, the gifts come in the form of love, service, and blessing from others. And they've gone beyond being mere recipients of others' thoughtfulness and selflessness—they have learned to bless others by becoming gift-givers themselves.

Scenic Outlook
Thirty
Leave a Legacy

My path is littered with attempts at a variety of jobs, careers, and home-based businesses. I couldn't find the balance. I didn't have the passion to be successful, because I couldn't throw my heart into the mission.

Everything changed when I had children. I found my purpose—to leave a legacy by being a role model to these tender lives. I wanted to be an example they could carry with them the rest of their lives. I became passionate about imparting to my children a hunger for God and a desire to live to please Him. I knew I had the privileged position in their lives to accomplish that mission.

Part of that mission involves defining success for my children—true success. Success means different

108

things to different people. The definition of success changes as our children grow and go through the various stages of life. When this journey started, I had a clear vision of success; however, during the previous years, I was blinded. I was a successful mother but didn't realize it.

We sometimes become confused by our culture's definition of success—money, fame, and position. God defines success differently—success is becoming all He created us to be. Success is not being distracted by money, fame, or position, but focusing on glorifying God and blessing others with our gifts and talents. God wants us to be successful in all the right things.

Martin Luther once said, "The less I pray, the harder it gets; the more I pray, the better it gets." Luther understood that success in life comes from letting God lead the way in determining how we should spend our time and gifts. True success comes after seeking the mind of God through prayer, Scripture reading, and yielding our hearts to His plan.

And so, the journey continues. This journey is never ending. The gifts keep going; the gifts continue to impact others after the initial experience is completed. A year has passed since the first gift was given to my daughter, and every day we discover new opportunities to be givers and receivers. We live in an environment of expectation—something unique and wonderful can happen today if we see the gifts around us and are willing to be gift-givers in our world. As we create and maintain an attitude of anticipation of God's goodness, our journey continues to enrich our lives and the lives of those around us. Our journey continues, and so does yours.

Be prepared, though. You will be changed. Your family will be affected, and your world will be touched. As you yield your life to the possibilities and opportunities that surround you, lives will be transformed. This journey to the ultimate dream, this path to gift-giving, is a beginning and an end—an end to life as you have lived it, distracted by temporal goals and urgent, momentary demands, and the beginning of life as a journey to the ultimate dream. Be blessed, my friend, as your journey continues.

Appendix A

Kenzie's Journal

The Gift of Giving

Today, I made one hundred handmade cards—each one of them is different and unique. I am going to give them with the meals I give to people who can't get out of their houses.

Today, I delivered eight meals with Ms. Anne. I met some nice people. I met Ms. Jewel, who shared with me what she thought was the most important rule in life, and that was something I already knew: treat others like you want them to treat you.

Another great story was when we delivered food to a man who had a heart transplant. He told me that he had a sixteen-year-old's heart in his chest and that was an awesome form of giving. To make it better, he shared that twenty percent of all recipients know their donors. He now has an extended family from the gift of giving.

All their stories were interesting and they all had something for me to learn about giving. They liked the cards I made because many of them never get cards like that.

I gave away some of my treasured bears today. It was both hard and easy. It was hard because I had them for a long time and they meant a lot to me. It was easy because I knew others would get them.

Lesson Learned: Giving something away made me feel valuable! We can all do something for others—draw a picture, give a hug, or throw a smile someone's way!

The Gift of Learning

I went to a camp over on the north side of town and met a lot of kids who go there for eight weeks to learn during the summer.

One of my favorite kids was a girl about my age. We played and hung out and she shared with me about her family. She told me that she lives with her aunt because her mom works a lot.

I met an interesting little girl who had trouble reading and staying still. I went and picked out a book; she sat by me on the couch, and we started reading together.

I also met really nice college kids who spend a lot of their summer teaching others. They do this every day all summer long.

I was given certain Scriptures to learn and am still studying them because I learned there are many more that can help me throughout my journey.

Lesson Learned: Learning is a privilege and I am thankful for the education I receive. I never looked at school as a gift.

We can even teach each others, though we are kids!

The Gift of Family

I saw a video today that my family was on. It was Grammie, Gege, Bea-Bea, Jamie, and my mom. They told me about some of their memories of family and growing up and about how we all need each other.

I watched the video on my way to the airport to fly to San Diego, California, to see my other grandparents. I never dreamed I would learn so much about family.

I stayed in room 316. The next morning, my mom and I walked on the beach and saw a tent with John 3:16 on the side. I asked why the tent was set up so early, and the pastor told me, "This is when the broken-hearted are here."

I saw many homeless people all around. They live on the beach next to the sea wall.

I met a man named William. He lives on the beach. We shared our story of why we are there. He told me he has an extended family that takes care of him, even though he doesn't have a home.

Lesson Learned: God provides us with an extended family, even when we have no one. Our friends and neighbors can be our extended family when we have no one.

The Gift of Work

Today I found out that I am going to work at a ministry that helps kids. We had to drive over an hour to get there because we got lost.

When I got there, I organized school supplies. I never knew that some kids don't have the money to buy their school supplies. I was glad to help.

I met a boy there who goes to school away from home. I didn't know that kids go to school away from home.

I got to eat lunch in the Senior Citizen Center. It was on a hill, and they get to eat there because some of them probably don't cook much.

I helped load boxes and move them to other buildings.

I worked hard throughout this whole journey. Sometimes I had to go and fulfill gifts when my other friends played outside or went swimming, but I wouldn't trade it for the world.

Lesson Learned: Work makes you feel really good! It doesn't always have to be a chore; it is a gift!

The Gift of Friends

We found out today that we are getting to go to my Grammie and Papa's house with my brother and my best friends for two days.

On the way we stopped and picked up Mady, my cousin. I love her very much and we have fun together. I am excited about staying at my Grammie and Papa's. I love them a lot.

We swam and played for two days straight and ate hot dogs and cake. The cakes at my Grammie's are the best.

My mom told us that friends are a gift from God, and that is a priceless gift you can give to anyone.

Lesson Learned: Friendship is priceless!

The Gift of Dreams

Today I found out that I am going to be given the gift of dreams. I have dreamed about this for over two years.

I am flying to Pennsylvania to meet my favorite superstar, Carrie Underwood, who I feel gave me the gift of dreams.

I almost passed out when my mom told me what I was going to do!

On the plane, my mom and I met this girl who lived near our town who shared with us that her mother needs a double-lung transplant. I wish I could've helped her; she needed money to get it done. I know, though, that someone will give her what she needs because of what I have learned on my journey.

I met Carrie and it was awesome. I also met a girl who had been sick and was getting her dream also. I wanted to give her more time with Carrie, so I told mom we needed to hurry so that her dream could come true.

Carrie is a gift. She teaches me that we can all dream and believe in ourselves. She has given me such a gift because I know that I can be anything I want to be.

I am thankful for people like Tony Romo. Even though he is a famous football player, he gives us the gift of dreams too. He teaches us to believe in ourselves and in our dreams because they do come true. I think he is a very humble person, and many kids look up to him. Anything is possible. Thanks, Tony!

At school one day, I drew a picture of a park with birds flying over. I picked the poem by Langston Hughes to put with my picture. This is the poem I wrote on the page with my picture:

"Dreams"
Hold fast to dreams
For if dreams die
Life is a broken-winged bird
That cannot fly.
Hold fast to dreams
For when dreams go
Life is a barren field
Frozen with snow.

At the bottom I wrote a note to my mom.
P.S. Keep working on your dreams. I'm working on mine. Kenzie.

I later gave it to my mom and she carries it in her Bible.

Lesson Learned: Dream big! Dreams do come true when you believe!

The Ultimate Gift

My family was all there: Grammie, Papa, Uncle Greg, Aunt Tonya, Mom, Dad, Luke, Gege, and Papa. Our friends were there too. I was really nervous about being in front of all my church family, but then we prayed, and I was excited to be baptized.

Mom went with me to the baptistery and helped me get ready, and my dad and Luke sat with my family so that they could film it.

It was beautiful from up there. I walked in the water, letting go of my mom's hand. I had butterflies in my stomach, but I was so excited to go under the water. When I walked out of the baptistery I felt like my new journey was just beginning!

It's really hard to describe in words. We gave all the kids who came to my baptism a guitar pick on a necklace that said, "Pick Jesus."

It was one of the best days of my life!

The ultimate gift is available for anyone! It is the best gift you will ever receive. Have fun on your journey in life—I know I am!

Lesson Learned: I found my ultimate gift—Jesus.

The End.

Appendix B

Breathe and Have Faith:
A Note from Sherri

Breathe and Have Faith

Someone recently described me as being rough around the edges. At first I was offended—I've never been described quite like that. But as I thought about it, I realized it was a compliment. In the beginning stages, a diamond is rough around the edges. Experiences in this country girl's life have polished those rough-around-the-edges parts of my heart to transform me into the country sunshine most people know.

I was able to encourage Heather and Kenzie on their journey to "breathe and have faith" because I have learned that lesson well in my own life. Things have not worked out as I planned. My first marriage ended in divorce, and so I was a single mom with two small boys. Life was hard. My parents helped me through those rough early years, but I was heartbroken when my daddy died.

I married my cowboy love, Gary. Several years later, my youngest son lost half of a kidney in a golf cart accident. Then my oldest son was severely injured in a boating accident—the propeller ran over him, leaving him fighting for his life and limbs. He survived, but he endured great trauma on his road to recovery.

More heartache followed—my Gary was killed in an automobile accident. His funeral was *Lonesome Dove* style—horse-drawn wagons and friends on horseback following behind. As I left the cemetery that day, I begged God for help. His answer came as

I sat alone on the back patio of our ranch home—
Daughter, I've loved you since I created you. I'm here.
Have faith.

Trusting and clinging to faith had been my
mainstay through the years, and here I was reminded
again that I needed to turn my life over to God—He
could be trusted, even when I didn't know the answers
or understand my pain. I learned anew to breathe and
have faith.

Rough around the edges? You bet. I've been
through so much—God has rolled me over and over
in His river of pain and trials, and in so doing, He
has polished me into His sparkling gemstone. I am
His. I can quickly offer this encouragement to others:
When things aren't working out as you've planned,
trust that God is in control. He has a wonderful plan,
and you can rest in Him . . . you can breathe and have
faith.

Appendix C

Study Guide—
Questions to Ponder on Your Journey

Journey Stop One
Experiencing the Gifts of the Journey

1. What are the most important gifts in my life?

2. How can I change the way I view gifts? What role do material possessions play in gift-giving? What lasting gifts do I want to give to my children? How can I make those gifts memorable?

3. Who are the gift-givers in my life? Who are the gift-givers in my children's lives?

4. What gifts do I have? What gifts do my children possess? How can I help my children to develop their gifts more fully?

5. How can I introduce my children to the ultimate gift: a relationship with Jesus Christ?

Journey Stop Two
The Gift of Giving

1. How do I feel when I give to others?

2. Who can I reach out to? What are their specific needs? How can I give to them? What can I do to make their lives better?

3. What material possessions can I give away?

4. What organizations can I volunteer for? Who needs a word of encouragement? Who can I write notes/cards to?

5. What conveniences do I take for granted? How can I live with a more appreciative attitude for the gifts given to me?

Journey Stop Three
The Gift of Learning

1. How can I be a better learner? What opportunities do I miss because I take them for granted?

2. How do the words of the Bible affect me? Do I let them transform me? Do I work to learn them and treasure them in my heart?

3. How can I teach others? Who is open to my input into their lives? What can I do to encourage others to learn and grow? How can I help others develop a love for learning?

4. How important is reading to me? Do I stretch myself by reading new and different types of books? How can I help others learn to love reading?

5. What kind of treasure hunter am I? What treasures do I pass daily without even noticing? How can I develop eyes to see the treasures that surround me, and how can I enjoy the full benefits of those treasures?

Journey Stop Four
The Gift of Family

1. How do I take my family members for granted? How can I change my behavior openly to express appreciation and love for them? How can I demonstrate to them that they are a gift to me?

2. How can I learn from those who have gone before me—parents, grandparents, aunts, uncles, and older siblings? What do their lives teach me?

3. How can I become "family" to those without family members? How can I make a difference in the life of someone who is alone today?

4. How can I invite others to become a part of the family of God? How can I introduce others to the family of God? What can I do to demonstrate the qualities of a child of God?

5. How important is the church? Who needs the church? How can I use my gifts within the church community?

Journey Stop Five
The Gift of Work

1. What can I do to help work not be boring? How can I adjust my attitude to make work more appealing?

2. What organizations near me need volunteers? What can I do? How can I contribute, even if I can't spend time at the organization's facilities?

3. How does interacting with the recipients of the gift make the job more exciting? How can I develop a caring heart for the recipients of the gifts? Can I put myself in their place—those individuals who are going without food, clothing, shelter, air conditioning, new toys, Thanksgiving meals, Christmas toys, etc.?

4. How do I look at homeless people? What attitudes do I need to change about those who ask for help?

5. How can I help others? How can I help my family? How can I give the gift of work today?

Journey Stop Six
The Gift of Friends

1. Who are my friends? Do I treat them with appreciation and thoughtfulness?

2. Do friends always agree? How should friends handle differences of opinions and points of contention?

3. How can friends step in and fill the role of family members?

4. How can I be a blessing to a friend today?

5. How does God view friendship? What Bible verses speak of friendship?

Journey Stop Seven
The Gift of Dreams

1. How do I limit God by limiting my dreams? Are my dreams big enough? Can I dream bigger?

2. Who has been behind the scenes in making my dreams come true? How does God use others to bless me? How can I be a behind-the-scenes blessing to someone else?

3. Do I allow myself to enjoy the dream—to revel in the moment and experience the fullness of joy at a dream come true? How can I relax and enjoy the process of getting to the fulfillment of the dream? How can I truly experience peace in the process?

4. When problems arise, do I give up on the dream? Do I allow obstacles to stall my dream? How can I become more persevering? How does endurance help? What can I learn through the obstacles?

5. What dreams do I need to reach for? What unexplored areas of life wait for me?

Journey Stop Eight
The Ultimate Gift

1. What is the ultimate gift?

2. What gift did Jesus give on the cross?

3. What is the most important decision I will ever make?

4. What is true greatness, and how do I experience it?

5. How can I lead others to the ultimate gift?

Thirty Scenic Outlooks
on the Journey to the Ultimate Dream

1. How can I change my perspective on life to see it as a gift-giving journey? How do I need to prepare my family and myself to make the changes that reflect the shift in our focus?

2. What gifts am I missing because I'm not looking for them? What opportunities am I missing to experience these gifts?

3. How can I put God first and keep God first today?

4. How can I seek God in my present circumstances?

5. What lasting gifts has God provided in my life?

6. What do I worry about? Am I emphasizing what's important to God? How can I change my perspective to see what's really important in my present circumstances? Is there anything I can release to God with the understanding that it just isn't that important in the whole scheme of things?

7. What has God said yes to in my life? What has He said no to? Can I rest in faith that He knows what's best at this time of my life? Am I willing to surrender those areas of my life that seem

unanswered, where God may be telling me to wait? What disappointments have paralyzed me in the past? How can those disappointments be used by God to make me more like Him? How might those disappointments be opportunities to see life from a different perspective? How can I embrace a change in plans and adopt the confidence that God is in control and cares about every detail of my life?

8. What material things do I try to substitute for the lasting gifts? Will I let God open my eyes to lasting treasures? What's really important in life?

9. What can I ask God today? How am I limiting the blessings of God in my life by not asking? What treasures await me in my world? How can I become a treasure hunter today?

10. Who is watching my life today and may be impacted by what they see and hear? Am I being a role model of God's goodness and graciousness?

11. What opportunities can I provide to my kids today to use their unique gifts and talents? Where am I uncomfortable in life? How can I reach beyond my comfort zone today?

12. How can I help my child reach for true greatness? What does greatness really look like? How can my children learn humility? How can I dream

big? What dreams wait for me? How can I make them happen? What dreams do I wait for God to deliver?

13. What am I thankful for? How can I change my attitude to be grateful for every lesson in life as well as every blessing? How can I be a blessing to every member of my family and thank God for them?

14. Who are the behind-the-scenes givers in my life? How can I show my appreciation?

15. Who are my heroes, extraordinary and ordinary? How can I encourage them and thank them? Am I a hero to my children, to anyone? How can I become a hero?

16. Do I have an attitude of availability? Am I willing to be inconvenienced? Who needs a friend today? What can I do to be a friend? Am I willing to be picked, maybe by someone I'm not comfortable with? Am I willing to be a blessing even though it may be difficult?

17. Who do I know that needs to know Jesus? What practical things can I do to make their lives easier? What service can I do to bless others? What work or labor of love can I offer? Are relationships more important to me than physical, material gifts? Who can I offer the gift of relationship to? Who needs me?

18. How am I robbing God of glory? What can I do to relinquish my grip on my pride and accomplishments? How can I turn the attention to God in every situation? What circumstances should I approach with an attitude to "breathe and have faith"?

19. What people in my life demonstrate humility? How can I learn from them?

20. What gifts are lasting, eternal? What "things" and "stuff" do I become distracted by?

21. Who are the gift-givers surrounding me? How can I express gratitude for them? What can I learn from them?

22. How can I best invest my time today?

23. Who has needs that are greater than my own? How can I put them first? How can I develop a more nurturing heart? What can I do to nurture others? How can I meet the unique needs of the individuals around me? Who do I look after? Who needs me? What can I do to enrich their lives?

24. Do I appreciate my mother? How can I show honor and appreciation to her?

25. Do I respect my father? How can I demonstrate my appreciation for him?

26. How can I be a safe place for my kids? Do I welcome the opportunity for my children to share their fears, failures, and mistakes? Do I respond in compassion and empathy? How can I give my children appropriate freedom to grow and mature?

27. What strategies can I develop to overcome hurdles in my life? How can I trust God more fully in the midst of discouragement and problems? How can I teach my children to overcome hurdles? How does perseverance resemble survival?

28. How can I become a gift-giver? What unique talents and gifts can I offer my world? Where can I volunteer? Who do I need to call today? How can I get my children involved?

29. How can I create a gift-giving journey for my child? How can my children grow through a gift-giving journey?

30. How can I leave a legacy for my children? How does God define success? What journey stops do I want my children to experience? How can I enrich their journey of life? How can they enrich others' lives with their gifts?

About the Authors

Heather Chabino lives in Tulsa, Oklahoma, with her husband, Doug, and their children, Kenzie and Luke. She is a stay-at-home mom and spends her free time volunteering at her children's activities and within her community. Heather earned her Associate of Natural Science degree from St. Gregory's University, in addition to a Bachelor and Master of Science in Speech Pathology from the University of Tulsa. Her contact information can be found at www.ultimatedreambook.com.

Sherri Watson taught elementary school and coached junior and senior high girls' softball and basketball for several years. For the last ten years, she has owned and operated a creative art business that sandblasts custom designs on glassware.

Sherri resides in Edmond, Oklahoma, where she enjoys spending time with her two grown sons. She attended Southwestern Oklahoma State University in Weatherford, Oklahoma, graduating with a Bachelor of Science in Elementary Education and Science and a minor in Physical Education. Sherri can be contacted at www.ultimatedreambook.com.